Credits

Producer/Food Stylist/Cover and Back Designer
Ethel Davis
336-491-5298
stylistdee@ymail.com

Food Stylist Assistant
Esther Barragan
704-737-7928
esther.carmenb@gmail.com

Photographer
D. Jonathan Hutchings
704-491-7415
www.djonathanhutchings.com

Typist
April Pate
Fatness12and3@hotmail.com

Senior Editor and Proofreader
Betty T. Morton
goodcook526@aol.com

Editor
Mitsi Smith
mrsfoodie@yahoo.com

Dedication

This is my second cookbook and it is dedicated to The Fresh Market managers and customers who have supported me from the beginning. Thank you so very much for believing in my first cookbook, *Comfort Foods of the South*. Without your continued support, this second book would have been very difficult to produce.

I would also like to dedicate this book to my favorite cousin, Alan J. Eason. He has been my biggest supporter. When I had doubts about my first cookbook being published, he supported me in every way possible. He also encouraged me to continue in the direction that I wanted to take my company.

On vacation in the summer of 2009, we got the opportunity to bond as a family. We had time to reflect on our lives and reminisce about the times we had as children. As we talked about the meals our family prepared, he gave me some great ideas about writing this cookbook. His father was a great cook from Savannah, Georgia. I can still taste those great ribs that we used to eat when we were kids. I only wish that we could remember how his father prepared his ribs. They were great. Thank you Alan for always being there for me.

Acknowledgements

I would like to acknowledge some very important people. Without these people this book would not have been possible.

But first, I would like to thank God for giving me the vision to write these healthy and simple recipes. I also thank Him for sending the following people into my life.

Next, I would like to acknowledge Ethel Davis for the great look that she gave to the front and back cover of my first cookbook, *Comfort Foods of the South*. She also styled some of the food in this cookbook. Without that great styling, I may not have been noticed by so many people. I loved her work so much that I am honored to have her produce and be the food stylist for my entire second cookbook, *The New South, Simple Healthy Southern Recipes*.

I would like to thank Betty T. Morton from Richmond, Virginia. Most of us know her from the Reynolds Wrap commercials, but may not know that Winston-Salem is her hometown. Her love of food and knowledge of it inspires me daily. She has helped me grow in so many ways. Additionally, she has been a great media coach as well as a recipe developer, senior editor and proofreader. She keeps me up to date on all of the latest food and lifestyle trends.

I would also like to thank April Pate for a job well done as typist. Her keen eye and attention to details has helped me greatly.

To my photographer, D. Jonathan Hutchings, thank you so much for taking some of the best photos I have seen. Your work will be enjoyed by so many people.

I would also like to thank Amanda Bazemore, the producer of "The Morning Show" on WFMY News 2 in Greensboro, NC. I thank you so much for giving me an opportunity to do cooking demonstrations on television. You have made one of my dreams come true.

Finally, I would like to thank Mitsi Smith for editing and giving me great advice putting this cookbook together. Her knowledge of printing books has made my job easy.

Introduction

The New South, Simple Healthy Southern Recipes is my second cookbook and I am so exicted about it! The title of this cookbook represents combining the concept of my first cookbook, *Comfort Foods of the South* with the concept that you can eat healthy food that is both beautiful and great tasting. Both cookbooks contain simple recipes that come from my passion for traditional southern comfort foods. You will find that I have updated some old classics and added my twist on some new favorites.

Now that I have created my own BBQ Sauce, there is a chapter on BBQ. My new sauce, Spice Delight Sweet & Zesty BBQ Sauce, is so delicious I had to bottle it! There are chapters on soups and salads, veggies and sides, as well as chapters dedicated to drinks and sweets. I am sure the entire family will enjoy trying these new recipes.

While the emphasis is on flavor and using fresh and seasonal ingredients, I felt it hugely important to focus on health as well. I have chosen some cooking methods that require very little fat. Salt and other sodium products are used sparingly. While there are many wonderful low-fat, low-salt and low-carbohydrate products available, I like every good cook, have my favorites. Please see my Chef's Notes page for these recommendations.

These recipes are quick, easy and versatile, allowing you the opportunity to create memorable meals in your own kitchen. I hope you and your family will enjoy this new contemporary style of Southern cooking.

Chef Barry Moody

Foreword

I was flattered when my "foodie friend" Chef Barry Moody asked me to write the foreword for his second cookbook, *The New South, Simple Healthy Southern Recipes*. Your taste buds will take a non-stop culinary journey when you try the recipes from this cookbook. Chef Barry is blessed to be able to live his passion by making and marketing high quality specialy spices and sauces for his Spice Delight brand. His love and appreciation for good food is deeply rooted in his cooking style based on his childhood memories of great meals prepared by his mother who was from Savannah, GA. We got a taste of his "so simple", as he describes it, style of southern cooking in his first cookbook, *Comfort Foods of the South*. He is also a "culinary lyricist", another one of his favorite terms, when creating new recipes for his cookbooks and cooking classes at Best Health in the Hanes Mall in Winston-Salem.

I met Chef Barry Moody at the opening night of the 2008 Kwanzaa Festival in Winston-Salem. He was one of the vendors that night, dressed in a unique and colorful chef's jacket standing behind his table. With a friendly, deep voice he spoke to everyone who walked by. For a special price, Chef Barry offered his *Comfort Foods of the South* cookbook and 2 bottles of his signature Spice Delight All-Purpose Essence. I was with my sister Linda Totten who knew Chef Barry from his demos and tasty food samples at The Fresh Market. She introduced us and he was surprised that Betty from the Reynolds Wrap foil commercials and Test Kitchens was a Winston-Salem native. I was pleased to meet an African-American chef, spice manufacturer and self-published cookbook author in my hometown. Both my sister and I bought 2 bottles of Spice Delight All-Purpose Essence and his cookbook, which he autographed. He told us the story of how he started making and selling his Spice Delight Essence and BBQ Rub. He was a true salesman, very engaging, enthusiastic, warm and very passionate about his products and his new cookbook.

Chef Barry told me that he wanted to introduce a unique barbecue sauce as his next product. He asked me if I could help him. I told him I have skills in copy editing and proofreading. After meeting at Kwanzaa, we became "foodie friends" and enjoy talking about food and recipes. It was a pleasure to find someone who shared my love of great food. Through emails, my "eagle eye" proofed and helped him finalize his new barbecue sauce label. In the summer of 2009, Chef Barry launched his Spice Delight Sweet & Zesty BBQ Sauce. It is another excellent product in his line.

Since our meeting, Chef Barry has introduced a barbecue sauce and launched his website, www.spicedelight.com. Another dream came true when a producer from WFMY TV 2 in Greensboro tasted his food at a demo at The Fresh Market. She asked him if he wanted to showcase his products and recipes on cooking segments on the weekend news. Of course he said yes and is now taping cooking segments for many weekend news shows on WFMY TV 2. I was happy to share my media training knowledge to help Chef Barry do on-air cooking demos. It has been a pleasure for me to be his media coach. He has learned the importance of smiling when on-camera and how to demo the recipe as if you are teaching your best friend.

You will enjoy the recipes in Chef Barry Moody's second cookbook *The New South*. Whether or not you have ever stood in line at The Fresh Market to taste his delicious samples made with Spice Delight products, you will want to add this cookbook to your collection. The recipes are healthy and palate pleasing. Some are, as he says, "quirky and whimsical", which is also his cooking style. Know that each recipe was created with passion and a love of great food and good cooking. Spice Delight products have become staples in my kitchen. You will want to have them all in your kitchen, too. You can buy Spice Delight products on his website and in The Fresh Market stores. Chef Barry often refers to himself as a "culinary lyricist" and the recipes in this cookbook sing simple, healthy and delicious. I look forward to cooking *The New South* recipes and I know you will enjoy them, too. This cookbook also makes a great gift for your family and friends. Remember to log onto www.spicedelight.com to order Spice Delight specialty food products and also for recipes, Chef Barry's videos and cooking tips.

Betty T. Morton
Former star of Reynolds Wrap commercials
Culinary Consultant, Cooking & Media Coach

Chef's Notes

When my recipes call for stock, I may have noted Better than Bouillon Brand stock base. Please feel free to use what you like, but I suggest the you use Better than Bouillon stock base for stock. It has a rich, deep flavor and is available in a variety of styles, including organic, low-sodium and vegetarian. Simply follow the directions on the jar to make the required amount of stock.

I also highly recommend Smart Balance Butter Substitute whenever a recipe calls for butter. It has a wonderful flavor and texture and is naturally low in trans-fats. This is a great heart-healthy butter alternative.

I hope that wherever you live you are able to take advantage of the local produce and seasonal items. It is so important for all of us, but especially for our children, to understand the benefits of a well balanced diet that includes fresh fruit and vegetables. Cook them as little as possible to retain color, nutrients and texture.

If you have not had the opportunity yet, please try whole-wheat pastas, brown rice and whole grain breads. They can be used in any recipe that calls for rice or pasta or bread. There are many benefits to a high fiber diet and these products add more texture and flavor to any recipe.

Finally, on the following pages, please see my list for items no kitchen or pantry should be without.

Pantry Essentials

These foods should be stored in a cool, dark pantry or kitchen cabinet. Store oils, herbs and spices away from heat and light. Store flour and sugars away from moisture.

Dried Herbs & Spices
Spice Delight All-Purpose Essence
Spice Delight BBQ Rub
Basil
Oregano
Thyme
Rosemary
Italian Seasoning
Garlic Powder
Ground Cinnamon
Ground Allspice
Ground Ginger
Whole Nutmeg
Chicken and Beef Stock
Chicken or Beef Stock Base

Staples
All-Purpose Flour
Granulated Sugar
Turbinado (raw) Sugar
Powdered Sugar
Brown Sugar
Dried Breadcrumbs
Cornstarch
Baking Powder
Baking Soda
Corn Muffin Mix
Chocolate (semi-sweet & dark)
Cocoa
Salt & Pepper
Vanilla Extract
Lemon Extract
Orange Extract

Oils
Vegetable Oil
Olive Oil
Sesame Oil

Dried Foods
Dried Beans (assorted types)
Dried Fruits (raisins, cranberries, apricots, figs)

Rice & Other Grains
Basmati Rice
Arborio Rice
Brown Rice
White Rice
Oatmeal
Quinoa
Millet

Canned Goods
Chopped Tomatoes
Sun-dried Tomatoes
Tomato Sauce
Tomato Paste
Whole Tomatoes
Red, Black and White Beans
Peanut Butter

Vinegars
Apple Cider Vinegar
White Vinegar
Balsamic Vinegar
Red Wine Vinegar
Rice Vinegar

Dried Pasta
Macaroni
Angel Hair
Egg Noodles
Fettuccine
Lasagna
Spaghetti
Couscous
Orzo

Breads
Whole-Wheat Bread
Tortillas (corn and flour)
Ciabatta

Produce (store in a cool, dark place)
White Potatoes
Sweet Potatoes
Onions (store separately from potatoes)

REFRIGERATOR

Remember to clean out the refrigerator periodically and use up or discard food past their expiration dates, half-empty jars of condiments and other products. Line vegetable bins with wax paper to make them easy to clean.

Milk
Eggs
Butter
Trans-Fat Free Margarine or Spreads
Bacon and Deli Meats (including turkey bacon)

Condiments
Spice Delight Sweet & Zesty BBQ Sauce
Ketchup
Mayonnaise
Mustard
Salsa
Soy Sauce
Worcestershire Sauce
Hot Pepper Sauce
Jellies, Jams, Maple Syrup

Produce
Assorted Fresh Fruits & Vegetables
Lemons, Limes, Oranges
Cabbage

Essential Kitchen Equipment

Good set of knives
Set of pots and pans
- 2 or 3 saucepans with lids, ranging from 1- to 4-quarts
- 6-, 10- and 12-inch skillets (one of these should be cast iron)
- 6- to 8-quart stockpot
- Baking pans or dishes (metal and glass or ceramic)
- 13 x 9-inch and 8-inch baking pans
- 9-inch round baking pans
- Round and square casserole dishes
- Cookie sheets
- Rimmed cookie sheets
- 12-cup muffin pans
- Large roasting pan, at least 2-inches deep
- 9- or 10-inch round glass pie plate
- 10-inch tube or Bundt pan
- 9-inch loaf pan

Microwave-safe dishes
Electric mixer, stand or hand
Food processor and/or blender
Wire cooling racks
Food slicer or mandolin

Utensils

Measuring cups (liquid and dry)
Measuring spoons
Tongs
Hand or electric can opener
Instant-read and standard bulb thermometer
Set of mixing bowls (including 1 extra-large bowl)
Assorted cutting boards
Silicone spatulas
Metal spatula
Pancake spatula

Kitchen scissors
Pizza cutter
Colander
Garlic press
Whisks (round and flat)
Vegetable peeler
Box-shape grater
Microplane grater
Bulb baster
Gravy separator
Kitchen timer

Notes:

Table of Contents

Chapter 1:
Soups & Salads

This chapter contains soups & salads that are also healthy and easy to make. Many of these recipes are starters for great meals or are wonderful as appetizers. Some of the salads with their flavorful dressings are also light and refreshing main dishes for lunch or dinner. Many of them lend themselves perfectly to the vegetarian diet. The use of fresh vegetables and bright greens make the recipes on the next pages family-friendly and delicious.

Chapter 1:
Soups & Salads

White Bean Soup with Kale & Tomatoes

This rustic soup will warm the body and soothe the soul. It is also packed with antioxidants.

Makes 4 to 6 servings

Ingredients
2 tablespoons vegetable oil
¼ cup chopped red onion
½ cup chopped carrots
2 tablespoons Spice Delight All-Purpose Essence
1 tablespoon dried thyme leaves
1 cup diced canned tomatoes
1 quart chicken stock
2 cups frozen chopped kale
2 cups canned white beans, rinsed and drained

Method
1. Heat vegetable oil over medium heat in a large stockpot.
2. Add the onions, carrots, Spice Delight All-Purpose Essence, thyme and tomatoes; stir to blend ingredients. Cook 5 minutes over medium heat.
3. Add chicken stock and kale; cook 15 minutes.
4. Stir in beans; cook 15 minutes longer or until beans are warmed through.

Tip
Serve with your favorite Artisan bread and a green salad to make a complete by low-fat and healthy meal.

Cream of Mushroom Soup

This hearty soup will warm the hearts of everyone. The soup is dedicated to Mrs. Marilyn of the Hawthorne Inn in Winston-Salem, NC.

Makes 4 servings

Ingredients
1 tablespoon olive oil
2 cups button mushrooms, chopped fine
1 tablespoon flour
1 tablespoon Spice Delight All-Purpose Essence
1 tablespoon Better than Butter Bouillon (brand) Chicken Base
1 quart low-fat half & half

Method
1. In medium size saucepan over medium heat, add olive oil and mushrooms.
2. Sauté 4 minutes or until mushrooms are tender.
3. Add flour, Spice Delight All-Purpose Essence and chicken base; mix well.
4. Slowly stir in half & half.
5. Continue to stir until mixture becomes creamy.
6. Reduce heat; simmer 20 minutes until soup thickens.

Tomato White Bean Soup

This hearty soup is a vegetarian meal.

Makes 4 to 6 servings

Ingredients

1 tablespoon olive oil
2 cups chopped onion
1 tablespoon Spice Delight All-Purpose Essence
1 tablespoon dried thyme leaves
1 cup tomato puree
½ cup tomato paste
1 quart vegetable stock, divided
1 (15 oz.) can white beans, drained and rinsed
3 tablespoons cornstarch
3 tablespoons water

Method

1. In a large stockpot, heat oil over medium heat.
2. Sauté onions with spices listed above 5 to 6 minutes or until onions arc soft.
3. Add tomato puree, tomato paste and ¼ cup vegetable stock, stirring until blended.
4. Stir in remaining vegetable stock until smooth. Simmer 15 minutes. Add rinsed beans to soup.
5. Dissolve cornstarch in water; pour in soup while whisking.
6. Simmer 5 minutes longer. Add additional Spice Delight if more seasoning is needed. Serve with your favorite bread.

Curry Potato Soup

Makes 4 to 6 servings

Ingredients
2 tablespoons olive oil
1 cup diced onion
½ cup chopped green bell pepper
2 cups Yukon Gold potatoes, with skin on, diced medium
1 tablespoon Spice Delight All-Purpose Essence
1 tablespoon mild curry powder
1 quart chicken stock
1 tablespoon flour
1 ½ cups low-fat half & half

Method
1. In large stockpot, heat oil over medium heat.
2. Sauté onions and bell pepper 5 to 6 minutes or until vegetables are soft.
3. Stir in potatoes, Spice Delight All-Purpose Essence and curry powder.
4. Cook 3 to 4 minutes. Whisk in flour. Gradually stir in chicken stock, whisking until mixture is smooth.
5. Stir in half & half until smooth.
6. Reduce heat; cover and simmer about 30 minutes. Serve with your favorite crackers or bread.

Seafood Chowder

This is my favorite chowder. It is sure to warm you on a cold day.

Makes 6 to 8 servings

Ingredients

2 tablespoons vegetable oil
¼ cup chopped red onion
¼ cup chopped celery
¼ cup chopped carrots
2 cups whole canned tomatoes, diced medium
1 cup frozen corn, thawed
2 tablespoons Spice Delight All-Purpose Essence
1 tablespoon dried basil leaves
1 tablespoon dried thyme leaves
1 cup tomato paste
1 quart clam juice or chicken stock
1 quart tomato juice
2 cups Yukon Gold potatoes, diced medium
1 lb. large shrimp, peeled, tails removed
8 small clams
1 lb. sea scallops, slice in half lengthwise

Method

1. Heat oil in a large stockpot over medium heat.
2. Add the next 8 ingredients. Cook 10 minutes, stirring occasionally.
3. Add tomato paste, clam juice or chicken stock, tomato juice and potatoes. Cook 5 minutes.
4. Add shrimp, clams and scallops. Cook 5 minutes with lid on until clams open up and potatoes are tender.

Salad Slaw

Salad slaw is a combination of salad and coleslaw. It's unusual but very nutritious and tasty.

Makes 2 to 4 servings

Ingredients
Salad
1 cup Nappa cabbage, cut in half, cut into thin strips
1 cup broccoli slaw (bagged)
1 head red leaf lettuce, diced medium
1 cucumber, peeled, diced small
1 cup red seedless grapes, cut in half
1 cup finely chopped fresh pineapple
Sweet & Zesty Dressing
2 cups Hellmann's mayonnaise
¼ cup apple cider vinegar
⅛ teaspoon dry mustard
½ cup brown sugar

Method
1. Cut all of the Salad ingredients listed in a medium size bowl. Toss gently to mix.
2. To make the Sweet & Zesty Dressing, whisk together mayonnaise, brown sugar, vinegar and dry mustard.
3. Add desired amount of dressing to your salad.

Tip
If dressing is too sweet, add a little vinegar, if not sweet enough add a little sugar.

Nappa Cabbage Coleslaw with Sweet & Zesty Dressing

Nappa cabbage has a much softer texture than green or purple cabbage. This slaw is light and refreshing; and has great flavor on a hot summer day.

Makes 4 servings

Ingredients
Salad
2 cups Nappa cabbage, shredded fine
½ cup grated carrots
2 tablespoons finely chopped fresh parsley
½ cup chopped red bell pepper
Dressing
2 cups Hellmann's mayonnaise
½ cup brown sugar
¼ cup apple cider vinegar
⅛ teaspoon dry mustard

Method
1. Place cabbage, carrots, parsley and bell pepper in a medium size bowl; toss to mix.
2. Place mayonnaise, brown sugar, vinegar and dry mustard in a small bowl; whisk until smooth.
3. Add desired amount of dressing to coat the salad, tossing to coat salad.

Orzo Pasta Salad with Pesto & Sun-dried Tomatoes

This is a great pasta salad that can be served hot or cold.

Makes 4 to 6 servings

Ingredients
2 cups orzo pasta
1 tablespoon diced red onion
½ cup pesto sauce
2 tablespoons coarsely chopped sun-dried tomatoes
1 teaspoon Spice Delight All-Purpose Essence
¼ cup freshly grated Parmesan cheese

Method
1. Cook orzo pasta according to package instructions. When pasta is done, pour it into an ice bath to stop cooking.
2. Drain pasta; place in a large serving bowl. Add onion, pesto sauce, sun-dried tomatoes and Spice Delight All-Purpose Essence; mix well.
3. To serve, garnish with Parmesan cheese.

Gourmet Salad with Yogurt Trail Mix Dressing

This salad dressing is sweet and tangy. It is an extremely kid-friendly salad. This salad is simple, healthy and good tasting. Whether you use trail mix or dried fruit, it adds great texture to the dressing.

Makes 4 servings

Ingredients
2 cups vanilla yogurt
1 tablespoon turbinado sugar (sugar in the raw)
¼ cup fruit and nut trail mix *or* 2 teaspoons each of nuts, raisins and dried
    cranberries
1 bag gourmet salad greens (I recommend a mix of baby lettuces or Mache)

Method
1. For dressing, in a medium size bowl whisk together the yogurt, sugar and trail mix.
2. Rinse and dry salad greens; toss with desired amount of dressing.

Gourmet Salad with Sweet & Zesty Dressing

This gourmet salad incorporates the crunch of the nuts and the sweetness that comes from the dry fruit in the trail mix. There are so many trail mixes to choose from, so have fun with the salad.

Makes 4 servings

Ingredients

<u>Salad</u>
4 cups gourmet salad mix
1 cup trail mix (your favorite)
½ cup peeled and diced cucumbers
Sweet & Zesty Salad Dressing to taste

<u>Sweet & Zesty Salad Dressing</u>
2 cups Hellmann's mayonnaise
½ cup raw brown sugar
¼ cup apple cider vinegar
⅛ teaspoon dry mustard

Method

1. Combine all of the salad ingredients above in a medium size bowl; set aside.
2. Combine salad dressing ingredients in a medium bowl; whisk until smooth.
3. To serve, add enough salad dressing to coat salad.

Farmers Market Pasta Salad

This pasta salad is made hearty and healthy with the addition of fresh vegetables. It's also very beautiful to look at.

Makes 4 servings

Ingredients
2 cups bow tie pasta, cooked per directions on box
¼ cup diced red onion
½ cup diced zucchini squash
½ cup diced yellow summer squash
1 cup broccoli florets, cut small
1 pint grape tomatoes, halved
¾ cup low-fat or fat-free Italian dressing
1 tablespoon freshly grated Parmesan cheese
2 teaspoons Spice Delight All-Purpose Essence

Method
1. Place cooked pasta in a large bowl.
2. Add vegetables, Spice Delight All-Purpose Essence and Italian dressing. Toss until everything is evenly coated with the dressing.
3. Garnish with Parmesan cheese.

Tip
Hard cheeses such as Parmesan and Pecorino Romano are naturally lower in fat than other cheeses.

Romaine Salad with Pan-Fried Pineapple

You will love this salad. It has a nice caramel flavor or pineapple that has been pan-fried in the raw brown sugar.

Makes 4 servings

Ingredients
Salad

1 cup peeled, cored, thinly sliced fresh pineapple

2 tablespoons raw brown sugar

2 tablespoons salted butter or butter substitute

4 cups romaine lettuce, cut medium

Dressing

2 cups Hellmann's mayonnaise

½ cup raw brown sugar

¼ cup apple cider vinegar

⅛ teaspoon dry mustard

Method

1. Sprinkle both sides of pineapple slices with sugar.
2. Heat pan with butter over medium heat.
3. Pan-fry pineapple 2 to 3 minutes per side until caramelized. Remove from pan and chop.
4. Toss chopped pineapple with lettuce in a large bowl; set aside.
5. Whisk dressing ingredients in a medium bowl.
6. Toss salad with desired amount of dressing.

Tip

Purchase peeled and cored pineapple to save prep time.

Wilted Spinach with Portabella Mushrooms

Makes 4 servings

Ingredients

1 tablespoon olive oil
½ cup baby Portabella mushrooms, slice thin
1 tablespoon thinly sliced red onion
1 teaspoon Spice Delight All-Purpose Essence
4 cups spinach
¼ cup Balsamic vinegar
½ cup grape tomatoes, sliced in half

Method

1. Heat oil in a large skillet over medium heat.
2. Sauté mushrooms, onion and Spice Delight All-Purpose Essence for 5 minutes.
3. Add spinach and cook for 1 minute.
4. Add vinegar and cook for 1 minute longer.
5. Garnish with grape tomatoes.

Wilted Lettuce with Balsamic Vinegar

A warm wilted salad with Balsamic vinegar is a salad that you will enjoy over and over again.

Makes 4 servings

Ingredients
2 tablespoons olive oil
1 tablespoon Spice Delight All-Purpose Essence
4 cups iceberg or your favorite lettuce, diced medium
3 tablespoons Balsamic vinegar
½ cup grape tomatoes, sliced in half
1 small cucumber, peeled and diced small
1 cup diced avocado

Method
1. Heat oil in a large skillet over medium heat.
2. Sauté lettuce with Spice Delight All-Purpose Essence for about 3 minutes.
3. Add Balsamic vinegar; sauté 1 minute longer. Spoon into a large bowl.
4. Garnish with grape tomatoes, cucumber and avocado.

Rotisserie Flavored Grilled Chicken Salad

The bold flavors of this grilled chicken salad will satisfy those who like spicy food.

Makes 4 to 6 servings

Ingredients

2 tablespoons Spice Delight All-Purpose Essence
1 teaspoon *each* dried oregano, thyme, basil leaves and blackened seasoning
¼ cup olive oil
1 ½ boneless, skinless chicken breast halves
¼ cup ranch dressing
4 cups romaine lettuce
¼ cup grape tomatoes, cut in half

Method

1. Mix spices and herbs listed above in a small bowl.
2. Rub olive oil on both sides of chicken.
3. Dust both sides of chicken with enough spice blend to coat evenly.
4. Cover chicken and marinate in refrigerator 30 minutes.
5. Heat skillet or grill pan over medium heat until hot.
6. Cook chicken in skillet or on grill 3 tc 5 minutes per side or until done.
7. Combine ranch dressing with romaine lettuce.
8. Top with cooked chicken, garnish with tomatoes.

Tuna Salad

Most tuna salad in the south has pickle relish, but this salad is sweetened with dark raisins. I give it some crunch with pecans.

Makes 4 servings

Ingredients
1 large can tuna in water
½ cup low-fat mayonnaise
1 tablespoon finely chopped celery
½ cup raisins
1 tablespoon turbinado (sugar in the raw)
½ teaspoon kosher salt or sea salt
Torn lettuce leaves (iceberg or romaine)
2 tablespoons chopped pecans

Method
1. Drain tuna; place in a bowl. Break up tuna with a fork.
2. Add mayonnaise, celery, raisins, sugar and salt; mix well.
3. Cover and refrigerate 1 hour. For best results, refrigerate overnight.
4. Serve on a bed of lettuce. Garnish with pecans.

Notes:

Chapter 2:
Vegetables & Sides

Remember to always eat your vegetables. Try to eat at least 3 to 5 servings a day. This chapter includes some of my favorite vegetables and side dishes.

Chapter 2: Vegetables & Sides

Poached Broccoli Medley

Poaching adds flavor with little fat. Be sure not to overcook your vegetables so they retain their color and nutrients.

Makes 4 servings

Ingredients

2 tablespoons olive oil or Smart Balance Butter Substitute
½ cup sliced button mushrooms
¼ cup diced red onion
¼ cup diced green bell pepper
1 quart chicken or vegetable stock
2 tablespoons Spice Delight All-Purpose Essence
1 teaspoon dried thyme leaves
2 cups chopped fresh broccoli

Method

1. In a large stockpot, melt butter substitute.
2. Add mushrooms, onion and bell pepper.
3. Sauté over medium heat 4 minutes or until veggies are tender. Remove from pan and set aside.
4. Add chicken stock, Spice Delight All-Purpose Essence and thyme to pan; bring to a simmer.
5. Add broccoli; simmer 5 minutes or until broccoli is tender. Spoon broccoli from pan into a serving bowl. Garnish with reserved mushrooms, onion and bell pepper.

Braised Green Beans with Tomatoes & Onions

Makes 4 servings

Ingredients

1 tablespoon olive oil
1 lb. fresh green beans, ends trimmed and cut in half
¼ cup thinly sliced red onion
½ cup canned diced tomatoes
2 tablespoons Spice Delight All-Purpose Essence
2 cups chicken stock

Method

1. In a large saucepan, heat oil over medium heat.
2. Add green beans and onion; stir and sauté 3 minutes or until onions are tender.
3. Stir in diced tomatoes, Spice Delight All-Purpose Essence and chicken stock. Lower heat to a simmer.
4. Cover and cook about 16 minutes or until green beans are tender.

Cauliflower Mash

This makes a great substitute for potatoes.

Makes 4 servings

Ingredients
1 medium head cauliflower, cored and chopped fine
1 ¼ cups chicken stock (Better than Butter Bouillon brand)
1 teaspoon Spice Delight All-Purpose Essence
2 tablespoons fat-free half & half, heated to a simmer
1 tablespoon olive oil

Method
1. In a large stockpot over medium heat, add cauliflower, chicken stock and Spice Delight All-Purpose Essence.
2. Cook 20 minutes or until cauliflower is tender. Drain cauliflower, reserving stock for future use.
3. Mash cauliflower with half & half and olive oil.

Sweet & Sour Red Cabbage

Makes 4 to 6 servings

Ingredients
2 teaspoons olive oil
3 cups shredded red cabbage
1 medium apple, peeled, cored, diced medium
3 tablespoons apple cider vinegar
3 tablespoons turbinado sugar (sugar in the raw)
1 tablespoon Spice Delight All-Purpose Essence

Method
1. In a medium size saucepan, heat oil over medium heat. Add cabbage and vinegar. Cook uncovered 20 minutes or until cabbage is tender. Stir often to avoid burning.
2. Add sugar, apple and Spice Delight All-Purpose Essence. Cook for another 5 minutes.

Sautéed Spinach with Mushrooms & Tomatoes

This is a heart healthy side dish with a double whammy of antioxidants. The spinach contains lutein and the tomatoes contain lycopene!

Makes 4 servings

Ingredients
1 tablespoon Smart Balance Butter Substitute
½ cup button mushrooms, sliced thin
1 tablespoon Spice Delight All-Purpose Essence
2 (9 oz.) bags fresh spinach
½ cup vegetable stock
1 cup tomatoes, diced

Method
1. In a large sauté pan, melt butter substitute over medium heat .
2. Add mushrooms and Spice Delight All-Purpose Essence.
3. Cook 5 minutes; stir in spinach and vegetable stock.
4. Cook an additional 3 minutes.
5. Remove from heat; fold in tomatoes. Serve immediately.

Sautéed Spinach with Mushrooms & Parmesan Cheese

Spinach is full of iron and only takes minutes to cook. It seems like a lot of spinach but it really cooks down.

Makes 4 servings

Ingredients
1 tablespoon Smart Balance Butter Substitute
2 tablespoons diced red onion
½ cup button mushrooms, sliced thin
2 tablespoons Spice Delight All-Purpose Essence
2 lbs. fresh spinach
¼ cup chicken stock
2 tablespoons freshly grated Parmesan cheese
¼ cup grape tomatoes, sliced in half

Method
1. In a large saucepot over medium heat, melt butter substitute.
2. Add onion, mushrooms and Spice Delight All-Purpose Essence; cook 5 minutes.
3. Add spinach and chicken stock; cook 3 minutes longer.
4. Remove from heat; stir in Parmesan cheese and grape tomatoes.

Acorn Squash with Maple Syrup & Cinnamon

This is a great winter vegetable to cook. The skin becomes soft and tender when cooked so you can eat the entire squash. However, if you prefer you may scoop the flesh out of the cooked squash and discard the skin.

Makes 4 servings

Ingredients
2 tablespoons Smart Balance Butter Substitute, melted
2 acorn squash, sliced in half and seeded
4 tablespoons pure maple syrup
2 teaspoons ground cinnamon
Sea salt to taste

Method
1. Preheat the oven to 350 degrees.
2. Place squash halves on a cookie sheet, skin side down.
3. Drizzle ½ tablespoon melted butter substitute and 1 teaspoon maple syrup on squash.
4. Dust ½ teaspoon cinnamon on each half of squash. Sprinkle with sea salt.
5. Bake 45 minutes to 1 hour. Squash is done when it can easily be pierced with a sharp knife.
6. To serve, cut into slices; place on serving platter or scoop flesh into a serving dish.

Green Bananas with Spice Delight All-Purpose Essence

Green bananas that have been boiled in the skin have a nice savory flavor and are a wonderful alternative to rice or potatoes. Bananas only get sweet when they turn yellow.

Makes 2 servings

Ingredients
2 green bananas
2 tablespoons Smart Balance Butter Substitute
2 teaspoons Spice Delight All-Purpose Essence

Method
1. Cut a slit lengthwise throught the skin from top to bottom.
2. Place bananas in a medium size pot and fill with enough water to cover. Bring to a boil and cook for 15 to 20 minutes or until soft. Remove bananas from water with a slotted spoon and allow them to cool just enough to handle.
3. Remove the skin from bananas and place in a medium bowl. Mash bananas; fold in butter substitute and Spice Delight All-Purpose Essence.

Greens with Andouille Sausage

Some of the most popular southern greens are collards, mustards and turnips. The Andouille sausage adds a great smoke flavor. Purchase them from the deli department, they will have more flavor.

Makes 4 servings

Ingredients
1 tablespoon canola oil
½ cup Andouille sausage, diced medium
1 cup chopped onion
3 lbs. fresh greens, roughly chopped
1 quart low-sodium chicken stock *or* more as needed
1 to 2 tablespoons Spice Delight All-Purpose Essence

Method
1. Heat oil in a large stockpot over medium heat .
2. Add sausage and onion; sauté 5 to 6 minutes until onions are tender.
3. Add greens, chicken stock and Spice Delight All-Purpose Essence.
4. Cover; cook 45 minutesto 1 hour or until tender.

Lentils with Andouille Sausage

Lentils are a low-fat, highly nutritious legume with a fresh nutty flavor. Andouille sausage is a wonderful, spicy smoked sausage usually associated with Cajun cooking. The combination is incredibly flavorful.

Makes 4 servings

Ingredients
2 tablespoons Smart Balance Butter Substitute
½ cup red onion, diced medium
½ cup carrots, diced medium
1 tablespoon dried thyme leaves
2 tablespoons Spice Delight All-Purpose Essence
½ cup Andouille sausage, diced small
1 quart chicken stock
½ lb. dry green lentils

Method
1. In a large stockpot over medium heat, melt butter substitute.
2. Add onion, carrots, dried thyme, Spice Delight All-Purpose Essence and sausage. Cook 5 minutes until sausage is browned, stirring often.
3. Add stock and lentils. Cook 45 minutes or until lentils are soft, stirring occasionally to prevent sticking.

Tip
If lentils are too thick, add more chicken stock to thin out.

Curried Rice with Green Onions

I make this great curry dish with Basmati rice. It makes a wonderful side dish with chicken, pork or fish.

Makes 2 to 4 servings

Ingredients
1 tablespoon Smart Balance Butter Substitute
2 tablespoons chopped green bell pepper
1 tablespoon chopped red onion
1 teaspoon mild curry powder
1 teaspoon dried thyme leaves
2 tablespoons Spice Delight All-Purpose Essence
1 cup Basmati rice
2 cups chicken stock
1 tablespoon green onion, chopped

Method
1. Melt butter substitute in a medium size saucepan over medium high heat.
2. Add bell pepper, onion, curry powder, thyme and Spice Delight All-Purpose Essence. Sauté 3 minutes
3. Add rice and stock. Cook for 30 minutes uncovered until rice is tender, stirring often to prevent rice from sticking.
4. Garnish with green onion.

Dirty Rice

This side dish is normally made with chicken gizzards and livers. I will use ground turkey to reduce the fat content.

Makes 4 to 6 servings

Ingredients

1 tablespoon Smart Balance Butter Substitute
¼ cup chopped red onion
2 tablespoons chopped green bell pepper
½ lb. ground turkey
2 tablespoons diced celery
2 tablespoons Spice Delight All-Purpose Essence
2 cups chicken stock (Better than Bouillon brand)
1 cup Jasmine rice

Method

1. In a medium size skillet over medium heat, melt butter.
2. Add onions, bell pepper, ground turkey, celery and Spice Delight All-Purpose Essence.
3. Cook 5 minutes or until turkey is cooked.
4. Add chicken stock and rice; cook 30 minutes or until rice is tender, stirring occasionally to prevent sticking.

Succotash Rice

I thought that rice would make a nice addition to traditional succotash.

Makes 4 servings

Ingredients

1 tablespoon Smart Balance Butter Substitute
½ cup chopped red onion
½ cup frozen lima beans
½ cup frozen yellow corn
1 cup stewed tomatoes, chopped fine
1 tablespoon Spice Delight All-Purpose Essence
2 teaspoons dry basil leaves
1 cup Basmati rice
3 cups vegetable stock

Method

1. In a medium size stockpot, melt butter substitute over medium-high heat.
2. Add onion and sauté 3 minutes or until tender, stirring often.
3. Add lima beans, corn, tomatoes, Spice Delight All-Purpose Essence and basil. Cook 5 minutes.
4. Stir in rice and vegetable stock. Bring to a boil. Reduce heat to simmer.
5. Cover and cook 25 minutes or until rice is tender and liquid is absorbed, stirring occasionally to prevent sticking.

Parmesan Rice with Mushrooms & Onions

This will remind you of Risotto but it does not take a lot of work to prepare.

Makes 4 to 6 servings

Ingredients

1 tablespoon Smart Balance Butter Substitute
½ cup baby Portabella mushrooms, sliced thin
2 tablespoons diced red onion
1 teaspoon Spice Delight All-Purpose Essence
1 cup short grain rice
2 cups chicken stock (Better that Butter Bouillon brand)
½ cup fresh grated Parmesan cheese

Method

1. Melt butter substitute in medium size saucepan over medium heat.
2. Sauté mushrooms and onion with Spice Delight All-Purpose Essence for 4 minutes until vegetables are tender, stirring often.
3. Add rice and chicken stock; simmer 25 to 30 minutes or until rice is tender, stirring occasionally to prevent sticking.
4. Once rice is cooked, fold in Parmesan cheese.

Curried Rice with Green Peas & Scallions

This dish reminds me of an Indian dish call Somosas, which are potatoes and green peas stuffed in a pastry shell.

Makes 2 to 4 servings

Ingredients
2 tablespoons Smart Balance Butter Substitute
2 tablespoons scallions, white part only, sliced thin (reserve green part for garnish
2 tablespoons Spice Delight All-Purpose Essence
1 teaspoon dried thyme leaves
1 teaspoon curry powder
1 cup Uncle Ben's long grain rice
2 cups chicken stock
1 cup frozen green peas, thawed

Method
1. Melt butter substitute in a medium size saucepan over medium high heat.
2. Add scallions, Spice Delight All-Purpose Essence, thyme and curry powder to saucepan. Cook 4 minutes, stirring occasionally.
3. Add rice and chicken stock. Bring mixture to a boil. Cover and reduce heat to low. Simmer 25 minutes or until rice is cooked and liquid is absorbed, stirring often to prevent sticking.
4. Add peas to pan; toss with rice. Continue to cook 5 minutes longer or until peas are heated through.

Pineapple Rice with Raisins & Pecans

This rice dish is light and flavorful with a tropical flair. It makes a wonderful side dish with grilled chicken or fish.

Makes 4 to 6 servings

Ingredients
1 teaspoon Smart Balance Butter Substitute
1 cup fresh or canned pineapple, diced small
1 teaspoon ground cinnamon
3 tablespoons turbinado sugar (sugar in the raw)
1 cup uncooked rice
2 cups pineapple juice
½ cup dark raisins
¼ cup finely chopped pecans

Method
1. Melt butter substitute in a medium size saucepan.
2. Add pineapple, cinnamon and sugar. Sauté 6 minutes over medium heat until pineapple is golden brown, stirring often.
3. Stir in rice, pineapple juice and raisins; bring to a boil. Reduce heat to a simmer. Cook for 25 to 30 minutes or until rice is tender, stirring occasionally to prevent rice from sticking.
4. Serve hot or cold. At serving time, garnish with pecans.

Dirty Mashed Sweet Potatoes

This side dish is so comforting. It reminds me of all the goodness in the best sweet potato pie. They are called "dirty" because you leave the skins on.

Makes 2 to 4 servings

Ingredients
2 large sweet potatoes
1 cup low-fat half & half
2 teaspoons Smart Balance Butter Substitute
1 teaspoon ground cinnamon
2 tablespoons brown sugar
⅛ teaspoon pure vanilla extract
⅛ teaspoon sea salt

Method
1. Cut off and discard both ends of sweet potatoes.
2. Place potatoes in a medium size stockpot; cover with water. Bring to a boil; cook potatoes 20 minutes or until softened.
3. Drain and place in a medium size bowl, with the skin on.
4. Heat next 6 ingredients in a small saucepan over medium high heat. Bring to a simmer and turn off the heat. Slowly add hot mixture to sweet potatoes while mashing. Stop pouring when you reach the desired thickness.

Dirty Mashed Sweet Potatoes with Orange Extract

This recipe is like my Sweet Potato Nuggets recipe from my first cookbook, but the potatoes are mashed instead of roasted.

Makes 4 to 6 servings

Ingredients
4 medium sweet potatoes
4 tablespoons brown sugar
½ tablespoon ground cinnamon
2 teaspoons salted butter, melted
½ teaspoon orange extract
1 pinch kosher salt or sea salt
¾ cup heavy cream or milk, heated to a slight simmer
½ cup raisins
½ cup pecan pieces

Method
1. Place sweet potatoes in a large saucepot. Add enough water to cover potatoes.
2. Bring potatoes to a boil. Cook 20 minutes or until potatoes are soft.
3. Drain potatoes. Cut off and discard both ends of each potato.
4. Place potatoes in a large bowl; add brown sugar, cinnamon, butter, orange extract, salt and cream or milk.
5. Mash or whip potatoes until smooth. Place potatoes in a serving bowl; top with raisins and pecans.

Cinnamon Dirty Mashed Sweet Potatoes with Orange Extract

Makes 2 to 4 servings

Ingredients
2 large sweet potatoes
1 cup fat-free half & half
2 teaspoons Smart Balance Butter Substitute
1 teaspoon ground cinnamon
2 tablespoons brown sugar
1 pinch sea salt
⅛ teaspoon orange extract

Method
1. Cut off and discard both ends of sweet potatoes.
2. Place potatoes in a medium size stockpot; cover with water. Bring to a boil and cook potatoes 20 minutes or until softened.
3. Drain and place in a medium size bowl, with the skin on.
4. Heat half& half, butter substitute, cinnamon, brown sugar, salt and orange extract in a small saucepan over medium high heat.
5. Bring to a simmer and turn off the heat. Slowly pour hot mixture into sweet potatoes while mashing. Stop pouring when you reach the desired consistency.

Southwestern Sweet Potatoes

This simple side is enhanced with my Spice Delight BBQ Rub. The smoky flavor works well with the sweet potatoes.

Makes 2 to 4 servings

Ingredients

2 large sweet potatoes
2 tablespoons Spice Delight BBQ Rub
2 tablespoons Smart Balance Butter Substitute
¼ cup low-fat half & half
2 tablespoons turbinado sugar (sugar in the raw)

Method

1. Cut off and discard both ends of sweet potatoes and peel.
2. Place potatoes in a large stockpot; add enough water to cover potatoes.
3. Boil potatoes 20 minutes or until potatoes are soft. Drain; place in a large bowl.
4. Heat butter substitute, half & half and sugar in a small saucepan.
5. Add mixture to potatoes with BBQ rub. Mash or whip potatoes until smooth.

Tip

Serve with chicken or pork.

Quinoa with Portabella Mushrooms and Red Onions

Quinoa is a gluten-free seed that is cooked and eaten like a grain. It is packed with protein and high in amino acids. Before cooking, rinse quinoa a few times under cold water to remove the bitterness.

Makes 4 to 6 servings

Ingredients
2 tablespoons olive oil
½ cup baby Portabella mushrooms, sliced thin
¼ cup diced red onion
1 cup quinoa, rinsed twice under cold water
2 teaspoons Spice Delight All-Purpose Essence
4 cups chicken or vegetable stock
4 tablespoons freshly grated Parmesan cheese

Method
1. Heat olive oil in a large stockpot over medium heat.
2. Add mushrooms and onion; sauté 3 minutes.
3. Add rinsed quinoa, Spice Delight All-Purpose Essence and chicken stock. Cook 10 to 12 minutes or until liquid is absorbed, stirring often to prevent sticking.
4. Garnish with Parmesan cheese.

Split Peas with Andouille Sausage and Rice

This one pot dish will have you coming back for more. The sausage adds a nice smoky flavor to this meal.

Makes 4 to 6 servings

Ingredients
1 tablespoon Smart Balance Butter Substitute
¼ cup diced red onion
¼ cup chopped carrots
1 Andouille sausage, sliced into ½-inch rounds
1 tablespoon Spice Delight All-Purpose Essence
1 quart chicken stock
1 cup dry split peas
1 cup cooked white or brown rice

Method
1. In a large stockpot, melt butter substitute over medium heat.
2. Add onion, carrots, sausage and Spice Delight All-Purpose Essence; cook for 5 minutes.
3. Stir in chicken stock and peas; cook 45 minutes or until peas are tender.
4. Fold in cooked rice and serve.

Tip
Purchase the cooked Andouille sausage from the deli department. It has more flavor.

Omelet Burrito Wrap with Salsa

This great tasting burrito wrap makes a complete breakfast.

Makes 2 servings

Ingredients
1 tablespoon green bell peppers, diced medium
1 tablespoon diced red onion
1 strip turkey bacon, diced medium
1 tablespoon mild salsa
½ cup Egg Beaters
½ teaspoon Spice Delight All-Purpose Essence
½ teaspoon Smart Balance Butter Substitute
2 (8-inch) soft whole grain tortillas

Method
1. Melt butter substitute in a skillet over medium heat.
2. Sauté bell pepper, onion and bacon 3 minutes or until bacon is crisp.
3. Add Egg Beaters and Spice Delight All-Purpose Essence to mixture and cook for a few minutes.
4. Once omelet is done, place half of mixture on bottom of each tortilla.
5. Start wrapping by folding in sides slightly.
6. Roll by putting thumbs under wrap and roll from bottom of wrap.
7. Keep seam side down so wrap will stay intact.

Cinnamon Raisin Cornbread

This cornbread tastes like cake. It uses a packaged mix to make it quick and easy.

Makes 6 servings

Ingredients
1 (7 oz.) Bag Martha White® Sweet Cornbread Mix
½ cup whole milk
3 large eggs
2 tablespoons brown sugar
2 teaspoons ground cinnamon
1 teaspoon baking powder
½ teaspoon vanilla extract
½ cup raisins

Method
1. Preheat oven to 400 degrees.
2. Spray an 8 x 8-inch pan with vegetable spray; set aside.
3. In a large bowl, combine cornbread mix with milk, eggs, brown sugar, cinnamon, baking powder and vanilla; mix well. Stir in raisins.
4. Pour batter into prepared pan.
5. Bake 18 to 22 minutes or until golden brown.

Tip
Although this cornbread is wonderful on its own, when it's done, you can drizzle maple syrup on top.

Notes:

Chapter 3:
Meats & Poultry

This chapter is one of my favorites. It features the star of the show, the entrée. Meat is an excellent source of protein, the leaner the better for us. Here you will find healthy and hearty dishes that include beef, pork and chicken. There are some one-pot wonders and some quick fix meals.

Chapter 3:
Meats & Poultry

Keeping Meats Tender

Keeping your everyday cut of meat tender and juicy is not hard if you follow a few simple rules. Start with the right thickness.

1. First, start with meat that is a ¼- or ½-inch thick.
2. Next, rub about a teaspoon of olive oil or canola oil on both sides of the meat.
3. To get great flavor, dust an even coating of seasonings on meat and marinate meat at least 30 minutes up to an hour prior to cooking. I recommend seasoning with Spice Delight All-Purpose Essence.
4. Most importantly, do not overcook your pork or beef and do not undercook poultry. Invest in a good meat thermometer and follow guidelines for checking internal temperature of meat to insure safe cooking that will produce juicy and tender meat. Go to http://www.foodsafety.gov to get more information on minimum safe cooking temperatures for meat.

Here are some great tips for cooking a turkey, standing rib roast or any other large cut of meat.

- When seasoning your meats, add olive oil to help the seasonings penetrate the meat.
- Follow guidelines for safe handling and cooking of meat. Go to http://www.foodsafety.gov for more information.
- Always preheat oven about 20 minutes prior to cooking.
- Before you place your meat in the oven, add about 2 cups water or chicken or vegetable stock in the bottom of the pan, the liquid will help keep the moisture in your meat.

Mustard-Peppercorn Flank Steak

The bold flavors of mustard and peppercorns enhance the great flavor of the flank steak.

Makes 4 servings

Ingredients

1 tablespoon crushed peppercorns
2 teaspoons Spice Delight All-Purpose Essence
½ teaspoon dried thyme leaves
¼ cup prepared mustard
1 lb. beef flank steak, fat trimmed

Method

1. In a medium size bowl, mix the first 4 ingredients.
2. Spread spice mixture evenly on both sides of flank steak.
3. Cover and marinate flank steak at room temperature 30 minutes.
4. Cook meat:
   To grill: Grill over medium heat 3 minutes per side.
   To broil: Broil steak 4 to 6 minutes.
5. Let steak rest 5 minutes to retain juices. Slice flank steak diagonally against the grain.

Mustard-Rosemary Burger

Rosemary and mustard is what I use on lamb, but this combination works great on burgers, too.

Makes 3 to 4 servings

Ingredients
1 lb. ground beef chuck
¼ cup prepared mustard
3 teaspoons Spice Delight All-Purpose Essence
3 teaspoons dried rosemary
1 tablespoon olive oil
Hamburger buns (your favorite)
Lettuce and sliced tomatoes

Method
1. Shape ground chuck into 4 flat burgers.
2. Combine mustard, Spice Delight All-Purpose Essence and rosemary in a small bowl. Spread mixture evenly on both sides of burgers.
3. Cover with plastic wrap.
4. Refrigerate 30 minutes to marinate before cooking.
5. Heat a skillet or grill pan over medium high heat until hot, but not smoking. Add olive oil and cook burgers until well done.
6. Serve on hamburger buns topped with lettuce and tomato.

Pan-Fried Ribeye with Peppercorn Glaze

Makes 2 servings

Ingredients
2 (6 oz.) beef ribeye steaks
1 teaspoon olive oil
1 teaspoon Spice Delight All-Purpose Essence
2 tablespoons canola oil
1 tablespoon red onion, sliced thin
1 tablespoon green bell pepper, sliced thin
½ cup beef stock

Method
1. Place ribeyes on a plate. Rub olive oil and Spice Delight All-Purpose Essence evenly over both sides of steaks. Cover with plastic wrap.
2. Marinate 30 minutes at room temperature before cooking.
3. Heat a skillet over medium high heat until hot, but not smoking. Add oil and pan-fry steak 4 minutes per side.
4. Remove steak. Cover with foil to keep warm.
5. Add peppers and onions to skillet; sauté 2 minutes.
6. Add beef stock; bring to a boil. Continue to cook until liquid is reduced by half, about 5 minutes. Season with Spice Delight All-Purpose Essence.
7. Reduce heat; let glaze simmer 2 minutes.
8. Drizzle sauce over steak and serve.

Grilled NY Strip Steak with Onions and Mushrooms

This grilled NY Strip Steak with onions and mushrooms is a wonderful dish to serve at a dinner party.

Makes 2 servings

Ingredients
2 tablespoons vegetable oil, divided
2 (8 oz.) NY beef strip steaks
2 tablespoons Spice Delight All-Purpose Essence, divided
½ cup thinly sliced red bell pepper
¼ cup thinly sliced mushrooms
¼ cup thinly sliced green bell pepper

Method
1. Rub 1 tablespoon oil on both sides of the strip steaks.
2. Dust 1 teaspoon Spice Delight All-Purpose Essence on both sides of strip steak.
3. Cover with plastic wrap; let marinate 30 minutes at room temperature.
4. Heat grill or grill pan until very hot. Grill steak 3 minutes per side for medium-rare steak. Remove from grill. Cover with foil until serving time.
5. To make vegetable topping: Heat remaining tablespoon oil in a large sauté pan over medium heat.
6. Sauté peppers, mushrooms, onions and remaining tablespoon Spice Delight All-Purpose Essence for 4 minutes or until tender.
7. Serve vegetables over steaks.

Italian Sausage Chili

The Italian sausage makes a great chili. Making your own marinara sauce is easy and so much better than store-bought.

Makes 3 to 4 servings

Ingredients
1 lb. sweet Italian sausage, bulk or links, casing removed
1 tablespoon olive oil
½ cup onion, diced small
½ cup green bell pepper, diced small
1 (32 oz.) can crushed tomatoes
2 tablespoons Spice Delight All-Purpose Essence
2 tablespoons dried basil leaves
1 teaspoon dried oregano leaves
1 bay leaf

Method
1. Heat skillet over medium high heat. Add sausage; cook until well done (no pink). Break into pieces with spoon while cooking. Remove meat with slotted spoon to plate; cover with foil. Discard fat from pan.
2. Return pan to stove. Add olive oil, onion and bell pepper. Sauté 5 to 10 minutes until tender.
3. Add tomatoes, Spice Delight All-Purpose Essence, basil, oregano and bay leaf. Simmer covered on low heat, 30 minutes or until flavors blend together.
4. Remove and discard bay leaf. Serve chili over pasta or on your favorite bun.

Tip
Add 1 small can cannellini beans, drained and rinsed for added fiber. Italian turkey sausage can also be substituted to reduce the fat.

Parmesan & Rosemary Crusted Chicken Breast

Makes 4 servings

Ingredients
4 (6 oz.) boneless, skinless chicken breast halves
2 teaspoons Spice Delight All-Purpose Essence
2 cups seasoned breadcrumbs
½ cup freshly grated Parmesan cheese
1 tablespoon fresh rosemary, finely chopped
2 egg whites, lightly beaten
1 tablespoon water
Vegetable spray

Method
1. Preheat oven to 350 degrees 15 minutes prior to cooking.
2. Dust chicken on both sides with Spice Delight All-Purpose Essence. Cover with plastic wrap. Refrigerate 30 minutes to marinate before cooking.
3. In a shallow dish, mix together breadcrumbs, Parmesan cheese and rosemary; set aside.
4. In a separate shallow dish, whisk egg whites and water.
5. Dip chicken in egg wash, then in breadcrumb mixture. Be sure to coat both sides evenly. Place on a rimmed cookie sheet.
6. Spray both sides of chicken lightly with vegetable spray.
7. Bake 30 minutes or until done.

Tex-Mex Chicken Burger

This burger is nice and spicy. It has been flavored with the Spice Delight BBQ Rub, which along with the chili powder has a nice Tex-Mex flavor.

Makes 4 servings

Ingredients
1 lb. ground chicken (dark meat)
1 teaspoon ground chili powder
2 tablespoons Spice Delight BBQ Rub
1 tablespoon olive oil

Method
1. Mix ground chicken with chili powder. Form 4 flat chicken burgers.
2. Dust Spice Delight BBQ Rub on both sides. Cover with plastic wrap.
3. Refrigerate burgers 30 minutes to marinate before cooking.
4. Heat a skillet or grill pan over medium high heat until hot, but not smoking. Add olive oil and cook burgers until well done.
5. Serve with your favorite buns or rolls and lettuce & tomato.

Tips
● Chicken burgers are also great on the grill. If grilling, wipe the grill grates with oil so burgers will not stick.
● To reduce the carbs in this recipe, eliminate the bread and make a lettuce wrap. Fill a large romaine lettuce leaf with a crumbled chicken burger, shredded Pepper Jack cheese, diced avocado and tomato. Roll it up and enjoy!

Chicken Vegetable Pizzas

This pizza will make kids love eating their vegetables. Save the leftovers and pack it in their lunch next day.

Makes 4 servings

Ingredients
2 cups pasta sauce (your favorite)
4 Ciabatta flatbreads, cut in half lengthwise
2 cups rotisserie chicken, pulled into strips
2 cups frozen California Normandy vegetables, cooked, drained
2 teaspoons Spice Delight All-Purpose Essence
8 slices Provolone cheese

Method
1. Preheat oven to broil.
2. Spread ¼ cup pasta sauce on a flatbread half. Add ¼ cup *each* of the chicken and vegetables. Sprinkle on ¼ teaspoon Spice Delight All-Purpose Essence on top. Top with a slice of cheese. Repeat with remaining flatbreads.
3. Place pizzas on cookie sheet. Broil a few minutes until cheese is melted.

Tip
Ciabatta bread is a flatbread originally from Northern Italy. If you can't find Ciabatta, there are a variety of flatbreads available at the grocery store. Pick your favorite.

Curry Chicken Burger

This is a great burger for those who like curry. There are so many curry powders on the market. Have fun trying the different kinds.

Makes 2 to 4 servings

Ingredients
1 lb. ground chicken (dark meat)
1 teaspoon dried thyme leaves
1 teaspoon curry powder
1 tablespoon green bell pepper, chopped very fine
1 teaspoon red onion, chopped very fine
1 tablespoon Spice Delight All-Purpose Essence
2 cups seasoned breadcrumbs
2 tablespoons olive oil

Method
1. Combine ground chicken, thyme, curry powder and vegetables in a medium size bowl.
2. Form 4 flat chicken burgers. Dust Spice Delight All-Purpose Essence on both sides.
3. Press both sides of each burger in breadcrumbs to coat. Cover with plastic wrap.
4. Refrigerate burgers 30 minutes to marinate before cooking.
5. Heat a skillet or grill pan over medium high heat until hot, but not smoking. Add olive oil and cook burgers until well done.
6. Serve with your favorite buns or rolls, thinly sliced red onion, lettuce and tomato.

Tip
You can bake this burger for 20 minutes in an oven preheated to 350 degrees.

Basil Chicken Burger

Chicken burgers are a great alternative to beef burgers. They are light and can be baked, broiled, pan-fried or grilled.

Makes 2 to 4 servings

Ingredients
1 lb. ground chicken (dark meat)
1 tablespoon Spice Delight All-Purpose Essence
1 teaspoon dried basil leaves
2 tablespoons olive oil

Method
1. Form chicken into 4 flat chicken burgers. Mix Spice Delight All-Purpose Essence and basil together; sprinkle evenly on both sides of burgers. Cover with plastic wrap.
2. Refrigerate burgers 30 minutes to marinate before cooking.
3. Heat a skillet or grill pan over medium high heat until hot, but not smoking. Add olive oil and cook burgers until well done.
4. Serve with you favorite buns or rolls and cheese, lettuce, tomato and dill pickles.

Lemon Tarragon Chicken

This is a light and refreshing meal.

Makes 4 to 6 servings

Ingredients
1 tablespoon olive oil
1 ½ lbs. boneless, skinless chicken thighs
2 tablespoons Spice Delight All-Purpose Essence
1 tablespoon dried tarragon leaves
Zest and juice of 1 lemon

Method
1. Preheat oven to 350 degrees.
2. Rub olive oil on both sides of chicken.
3. Mix the Spice Delight All-Purpose Essence, tarragon and lemon zest together. Sprinkle an even coating of the mixture on both sides of chicken. Cover with plastic wrap.
4. Refrigerate chicken 15 to 30 minutes to marinate before cooking.
5. Bake chicken 30 minutes *or* grill 8 to 10 minutes per side over medium high heat until done.
6. Remove chicken to a serving platter; squeeze lemon juice on top.

Glazed Chicken Wings

Wings are great to serve for parties and everyday meals. With this glaze, your family and friends will be coming back for more.

Makes 6 to 8 servings

Ingredients

3 lbs. Chicken wings or drummettes
2 tablespoons Spice Delight All-Purpose Essence
½ cup orange juice
½ cup pineapple juice
½ cup low-sodium soy sauce
½ cup honey
1 tablespoon minced fresh ginger
1 tablespoon cornstarch
1 tablespoon cold water
Celery sticks
Your favorite dipping sauce

Method

1. Preheat oven to 400 degrees 15 minutes before cooking.
2. In a large bowl, sprinkle wings with Spice Delight All-Purpose Essence. Cover with plastic wrap. Marinate 30 minutes in refrigerator before cooking.
3. Meanwhile, prepare glaze. In a medium size saucepan over medium heat, bring next 5 ingredients to a slight boil. Cook 5 minutes.
4. Dissolve cornstarch in water.
5. Pour mixture slowly into boiling sauce while whisking.
6. Stop pouring when desired thickness is reached. If it gets too thick, thin it out with a little more juice or water.
7. Bake wings on 2 large rimmed cookie sheets 30 minutes or until done.
8. Place cooked wings into a large mixing bowl.
9. Pour glaze over wings; toss to coat. Do this in batches if necessary. Serve with celery sticks and dipping sauce.

Chicken Quesadillas

These fun quesadillas are nice and spicy and with the addition of the Pepper Jack cheese they have just the right kick.

Makes 4 servings

Ingredients
2 cooked rotisserie chicken breasts
½ cup green bell pepper, diced small
½ cup tomatoes, diced small
½ cup red onion, diced small
1 tablespoon Spice Delight All-Purpose Essence
4 (8-inch) flour tortillas
½ cup shredded Pepper Jack cheese
Low-fat sour cream
Salsa (your favorite)

Method
1. Pull chicken off the bone; place in a medium size bowl. Add bell pepper, tomatoes, onion and Spice Delight All-Purpose Essence; mix together.
2. Spread half of the chicken-vegetable mixture on a tortilla. Sprinkle on ½ of the cheese. Top with the other tortilla. Repeat with remaining tortillas.
3. Coat a large skillet with non-stick cooking spray.
4. Cook quesadillas over medium heat 3 minutes per side until quesadillas are golden and cheese is melted. Let tortillas rest 2 minutes before cutting.
5. Cut quesadillas into 4 pieces. Serve with sour cream and salsa.

Baked Ham with Pineapple Glaze

Ham isn't just for Sundays and holidays. This recipe makes Sunday supper into an easy weeknight meal.

Makes 4 to 6 servings

Ingredients
2 lbs. sliced ham
2 cups pineapple juice
1 cup fresh pineapple, diced small
2 tablespoons turbinado sugar (sugar in the raw)
1 teaspoon ground cinnamon
2 tablespoons cornstarch
2 tablespoons cold water

Method
1. Preheat oven to 350 degrees.
2. Shingle (overlap) ham slices in ovenproof dish; set aside.
3. Place pineapple juice, pineapple, sugar and cinnamon in a medium size saucepan.
4. Bring mixture to slight simmer for 3 minutes.
5. Mix cornstarch with water; pour into pineapple glaze while whisking.
6. Pour thickened glaze over ham. Cover with foil.
7. Bake 30 minutes.

Pork Tenderloins with Apricot Glaze

When I was a kid, my mother roasted her duck with this great glaze. Pork tenderloins cook quickly but are very tender and juicy. The combination is an elegant and easy main entrée.

Makes 4 to 6 servings

Ingredients
1 cup apricot preserves
2 tablespoons cider vinegar
2 tablespoons Spice Delight BBQ Rub, divided
1 tablespoon olive oil
1 pork tenderloin (about 1 to 1 ½ lbs.)

Method
1. Preheat oven to 350 degrees 15 minutes prior to cooking.
2. In a medium size saucepan, add the apricot preserves, vinegar and 1 tablespoon Spice Delight BBQ Rub. Heat over medium heat, whisking until glaze is smooth. If glaze is too thick add a little water to thin out. Set aside.
3. Rub pork with olive oil; dust the entire piece with remainder of Spice Delight BBQ Rub. Place on rimmed cookie sheet.
4. Cover with plastic wrap. Let marinate in refrigerator 45 minutes.
5. Bake tenderloin 25 to 35 minutes or until tender. Let rest 10 minutes before slicing.
6. Spoon glaze over sliced pork tenderloins.

Oven Baked Pork Burger

Makes 4 servings

Ingredients

2 lbs. ground pork
2 tablespoons prepared mustard
1 tablespoon poultry seasoning
2 teaspoons Spice Delight All-Purpose Essence

Method

1. Preheat oven to 350 degrees 15 minutes before cooking.
2. Form 8 flat pork burgers.
3. Combine mustard, Spice Delight All-Purpose Essence and poultry seasoning in a small bowl. Spread on both sides of burgers. Cover with plastic wrap.
4. Refrigerate burgers 30 minutes to marinate before cooking.
5. Place burgers on a rimmed cookie sheet.
6. Bake 18 to 20 minutes or until done.

Tip

Place ¼ cup water on the bottom of rimmed cookie sheet to help keep burgers moist during baking.

Chicken Sausage Hoagie

This hoagie is for people who don't eat pork or beef.

Makes 4 to 6 servings

Ingredients

1 tablespoon olive oil
2 lbs. chicken sausage, sliced ½-inch thick
1 tablespoon Spice Delight All-Purpose Essence
½ cup onion, sliced thin
½ cup green bell pepper, sliced thin
2 cups pasta sauce (your favorite)
4 to 6 French or Italian rolls

Method

1. Heat oil in a large skillet over medium heat.
2. Add sausage and Spice Delight All-Purpose Essence to skillet.
3. Cook 3 minutes, turning occasionally.
4. Add onion and bell pepper. Stir and cook 3 minutes longer.
5. Add pasta sauce.
6. Turn down heat to simmer; cook for 5 minutes or until sausage is done.
7. Serve on rolls.

Parmesan Turkey Burger

This is a simple and healthy way to cook turkey burgers. Oven baking eliminates having to use oil.

Makes 4 servings

Ingredients
Burger
1 lb. ground turkey
¼ cup freshly grated Parmesan cheese
1 teaspoon ground sage
1 teaspoon dried thyme leaves
1 tablespoon Spice Delight All-Purpose Essence
2 cups panko breadcrumbs
1 sheet parchment paper
4 Ciabatta rolls
Toppings
1 cup arugula
2 slices tomato
2 slices red onions
2 slices yellow bell pepper

Method
1. Preheat oven to 350 degrees.
2. Place all burger ingredients except rolls and panko breadcrumbs in a large bowl; mix together.
3. Make 4 flat turkey burgers; coat with panko breadcrumbs. Place on a rimmed cookie sheet lined with parchment paper.
4. Bake for 20 to 25 minutes or until burgers are done. Place burger on Ciabatta rolls. Garnish burger with toppings.

Mustard-Rosemary Lamb Tenderloin

This is a simple and healthy way to cook turkey burgers. Oven baking eliminates having to use oil.

Makes 2 servings

Ingredients
6 (2 oz.) lamb tenderloins
1 tablespoon olive oil
2 teaspoons Spice Delight All-Purpose Essence
2 teaspoons whole grain mustard
2 teaspoons dried rosemary
1 sheet parchment paper

Method
1. Rinse lamb tenderloins; pat dry.
2. In a small bowl, combine oil, Spice Delight All-Purpose Essence, mustard and rosemary. Stir into a paste. Use a spoon to spread evenly over lamb tenderloins.
3. Cover lamb with plastic wrap; let marinate in refrigerator for 1 hour prior to cooking.
4. Heat a non-stick skillet to medium high heat.
5. Sauté lamb 3 minutes per side. Cover with foil and let stand 3 minutes before slicing.
6. Slice and serve immediately.

Notes:

Chapter 4:
Spice Delight BBQ

I love BBQ sauce. Ever since I was a kid, I've loved all types of BBQ sauce. When I first started my spice company, I did not have a BBQ sauce. During my demos I used all the brands of BBQ sauces that were available. There were a lot of good ones out there, but none stood out as being very different. Some had a vinegary flavor, some had heat and some had hickory and sweetness. I wanted to create something that was different that what was on the market, so I created my own Spice Delight Sweet & Zesty BBQ Sauce. This great sauce is a combination of my favorite sauces with some fruity notes. In this chapter I have created some simple recipes that you and your family can enjoy.

Chapter 4:
Spice Delight BBQ

BBQ Hawaiian Chicken

This chicken features my Spice Delight Sweet & Zesty BBQ Sauce with fresh pineapple.

Makes 4 servings

Ingredients

1 lb. skinless, boneless chicken breast halves
1 teaspoon Spice Delight BBQ Rub
1 tablespoon olive oil
1 cup Spice Delight Sweet & Zesty BBQ Sauce
½ cup fresh diced pineapple
2 tablespoons cornstarch
2 tablespoons spring water

Method

1. Heat oven to 350 degrees.
2. Butterfly chicken breasts or pound until they are thin and flat.
3. Rub olive oil and Spice Delight BBQ Rub on both sides of chicken. Cover and marinate in refrigerator 30 minutes.
4. Place chicken in a baking pan and bake for 20 minutes or until done.
5. Heat Spice Delight Sweet & Zesty BBQ Sauce and pineapple in a medium size saucepan over medium heat.
6. Mix cornstarch with water in a small bowl. When sauce starts to boil, pour cornstarch mixture into sauce while stirring. When you get to your desired thickness, stop pouring. Boil 2 minutes longer.
7. Top chicken with BBQ glaze.

Tip

Place chicken between 2 sheets of parchment paper or plastic wrap to pound it out.

Pan-Fried BBQ Skirt Steak

Beef skirt steaks are so thin that they only take minutes to cook. They work well in wraps or on top of a salad.

Makes 4 servings

Ingredients
1 lb. beef skirt steak
1 tablespoon olive oil
2 tablespoons Spice Delight BBQ Rub
½ cup Spice Delight Sweet & Zesty BBQ Sauce

Method
1. Trim excess fat from steak.
2. Rub both sides of steak with olive oil.
3. Dust both sides evenly with Spice Delight BBQ Rub. Cover with plastic wrap.
4. Let marinate at room temperature 30 minutes before cooking.
5. Heat cast iron or non-stick skillet over medium heat.
6. Pan-fry steak 2 minutes on first side.
7. Turn over; let cook 2 minutes on second side.
8. Add Spice Delight Sweet & Zesty BBQ Sauce; cook 1 minute longer.

Tip
Serve over bed of lettuce for a quick salad. Garnish with tomatoes and cucumbers.
Make a quick wrap sandwich with a flour tortilla, Nappa Cabbage Coleslaw, thinly sliced onions and red bell pepper.

BBQ Turkey Meatballs

This recipe is perfect for parties. These meatballs are lower in fat than traditional meatballs and the flavor is outstanding.

Makes 6 servings

Ingredients
1 lb. Ground turkey breast (99% Fat Free)
1 tablespoon onion, diced small
1 tablespoon green pepper, diced small
1 tablespoon Spice Delight BBQ Rub
½ cup plain breadcrumbs
1 egg, beaten
1 cup Spice Delight Sweet & Zesty BBQ Sauce

Method
1. Preheat oven to 350 degrees.
2. In a medium size bowl, mix all ingredients listed above except BBQ sauce.
3. Form 12 medium size meatballs; placed on a rimmed cookie sheet.
4. Bake 20 minutes or until fully cooked.
5. Place meatballs in serving bowl. Pour Spice Delight Sweet & Zesty BBQ Sauce on top.

Tip
You can brown meatballs in skillet and place them in a slow cooker with 2 cups BBQ Sauce. Cook over high heat for 1 hour.

BBQ Pineapple Sauce

Pineapple and BBQ sauce makes an excellent topping for fish and chicken. The light and refreshing flavor will make you feel like summer all year long.

Makes 4 to 6 servings

Ingredients
1 tablespoon Smart Balance Butter Substitute
1 cup fresh pineapple, peeled, cored, diced small
1 cup Spice Delight Sweet & Zesty BBQ Sauce

Method
1. Melt butter substitute in a medium size saucepan over medium heat.
2. Sauté pineapple until it becomes caramelized.
3. Add Spice Delight Sweet & Zesty BBQ Sauce; simmer 10 minutes.

Tip
If you want to make a thicker glaze, mix 2 tablespoons cornstarch with 2 tablespoons cold water. Pour this mixture into simmering sauce while stirring. Stop pouring when you get to desired thickness.

BBQ Shrimp

The combo of the Spice Delight BBQ Rub and the Spice Delight Sweet & Zesty BBQ Sauce will make this one of your favorite shrimp dishes. Whenever it's possible, buy USA Wild Caught Shrimp.

Makes 5 to 6 servings

Ingredients
24 large shrimp, peeled and deveined
1 tablespoon olive oil
2 tablespoons Spice Delight BBQ Rub
½ cup Spice Delight Sweet & Zesty BBQ Sauce

Method
1. Place shrimp in a medium size bowl.
2. Drizzle with oil; sprinkle Spice Delight BBQ Rub onto shrimp.
3. Mix well so that rub and oil evenly coats shrimp. Cover with plastic wrap.
4. Let marinate 30 minutes in refrigerator.
5. Heat oil in skillet over medium heat.
6. Pan-fry shrimp 2 minutes per side. Pour Spice Delight Sweet & Zesty BBQ Sauce over shrimp, cook 1 minute longer in sauce.

Tip
To grill, heat grill to medium. Thread shrimp on a metal skewer. Grill 2 minutes per side. Brush with BBQ sauce and grill 1 minute longer.

BBQ Shrimp Skewers with Pineapple, Peppers & Onions

Serve this dish with the BBQ rice or Rice Pilaf.

Makes 4 servings

Ingredients
8 large shrimp, peeled and deveined
2 tablespoons olive oil
2 tablespoons Spice Delight BBQ Rub
½ whole fresh pineapple, peeled, cored, diced in ½-inch cubes
1 large green bell pepper, diced large
1 large red onion, diced large
½ cup Spice Delight Sweet & Zesty BBQ Sauce

Method
1. Place shrimp, oil and Spice Delight BBQ Rub in a medium size bowl.
2. Mix well so that oil and BBQ rub evenly coat shrimp. Cover with plastic wrap.
3. Let marinate 30 minutes in refrigerator.
4. Thread shrimp, pineapple, bell pepper and onion onto 2 metal skewers, alternating the ingredients.
5. Grill over medium heat 3 minutes per side.
6. Brush with Spice Delight Sweet & Zesty BBQ Sauce during the last 2 minutes of cooking. Discard any leftover BBQ sauce.

BBQ Salmon

Salmon is a bold-flavored fish that can take the zesty flavors of the Spice Delight BBQ Rub and the Spice Delight Sweet & Zesty BBQ Sauce.

Makes 2 to 4 servings

Ingredients

2 (8 oz.) salmon filets
1 tablespoon olive oil
2 teaspoons Spice Delight BBQ Rub
¼ cup Spice Delight Sweet & Zesty BBQ Sauce

Method

1. Heat broiler for a few minutes.
2. Rinse salmon; pat dry.
3. Rub oil on both sides of the fish. Sprinkle evenly with Spice Delight BBQ Rub.
4. Cover with plastic wrap. Let marinate in refrigerator at least 30 minutes.
5. Place salmon on non-stick rimmed cookie sheet or shallow baking pan.
6. Place pan on middle rack; broil 5 minutes.
7. Brush top surface with BBQ sauce; broil for another 3 minutes.

Tip

When broiling or baking, pour about ¼ cup water on rimmed cookie sheet to help keep moisture in foods.

BBQ Coleslaw

This recipe combines the Nappa Cabbage Coleslaw with my Spice Delight Sweet & Zesty BBQ Sauce.

Makes 4 to 6 servings

Ingredients
Coleslaw
2 cups Nappa Cabbage, shredded fine
½ cup grated carrots
2 tablespoons fresh parsley, minced fine
½ cup red bell pepper, diced small
Dressing
2 cups Hellmann's mayonnaise
½ cup packed brown sugar
¼ cup apple cider vinegar
¼ cup Spice Delight Sweet & Zesty BBQ Sauce
¼ teaspoon dry mustard

Method
1. For coleslaw, place cabbage, carrots, parsley and bell pepper in a medium size bowl; toss to mix.
2. For dressing, place mayonnaise, brown sugar, vinegar, Spice Delight Sweet & Zesty BBQ Sauce and dry mustard in another small bowl; whisk until smooth.
3. Mix in desired amount of dressing to coat the coleslaw.

Tip
Serve on hot dogs, hamburgers, grilled chicken wraps and pulled pork sandwiches.

BBQ Hot Dog

This American classic takes on southern flavor with BBQ sauce and coleslaw.

Makes 6 to 8 servings

Ingredients

1 package all-beef hot dogs
½ cup Spice Delight Sweet & Zesty BBQ Sauce
Hot dog rolls or hoagie buns
1 cup BBQ Coleslaw

Method

1. Slice hot dogs in half.
2. Grill or pan-fry a few minutes per side until crispy.
3. Brush hot dogs with Spice Delight Sweet & Zesty BBQ Sauce.
4. Serve on your favorite roll or bun with the BBQ Coleslaw.

BBQ Baked Beans

Baked beans are a great addition to any summer meal.

Makes 3 or 4 servings

Ingredients
1 tablespoon olive oil
1 small onion, diced
2 slices turkey bacon, diced medium
1 can (16 oz.) kidney or red beans, drained
¼ cup low-sodium chicken stock
½ cup Spice Delight Sweet & Zesty BBQ Sauce

Method
1. Heat oil in a medium saucepan over medium heat.
2. Sauté onion 3 to 5 minutes or until tender.
3. Add turkey bacon; cook 3 minutes.
4. Stir in beans, chicken stock and Spice Delight Sweet & Zesty BBQ Sauce; cook 20 minutes longer, stirring occasionally.

BBQ Rub Sweet Potatoes

North Carolina is one of the leading states for sweet potatoes. This sweet and savory recipe is a new twist on sweet potatoes.

Makes 4 to 6 servings

Ingredients

2 medium size sweet potatoes
1 tablespoon olive oil
2 tablespoons Spice Delight BBQ Rub
1 tablespoon brown sugar

Method

1. Preheat oven to 350 degrees.
2. Slice sweet potatoes into ¼- to ½-inch thin slices.
3. Drizzle oil onto a non-stick rimmed cookie sheet.
4. Spread sweet potatoes out onto cookie sheet.
5. Sprinkle both sides of sweet potatoes with Spice Delight BBQ Rub and brown sugar.
6. Bake 35 to 45 minutes or until potatoes are soft.

BBQ Pork Burger

The BBQ Pork Burger should have been the original Carolina Burger since pork is a very popular meat in North Carolina.

Makes 6 servings

Ingredients
2 lbs. ground pork
3 tablespoons Spice Delight BBQ Rub
½ cup Spice Delight Sweet & Zesty BBQ Sauce
1 tablespoon canola oil
Your favorite burger bun

Method
1. Make 6 flat pork burgers; sprinkle Spice Delight BBQ Rub on both sides. Cover with plastic wrap.
2. Let marinate in refrigerator 30 minutes.
3. Pan-fry in oil or grill over medium heat 3 minutes per side until done.
4. Pour Spice Delight Sweet & Zesty BBQ Sauce on top; serve on your favorite bun.

Tip
Try serving this BBQ Pork Burger with my Spicy Chipotle Mayo in the Sauces & Condiments chapter.

BBQ Country-Style Boneless Ribs

Country-style ribs are normally made from a pork butt or shoulder. I am using a tender, less fatty cut of meat, which is the pork tenderloin. This cuts the cooking time significantly making this recipe another easy weeknight meal.

Makes 6 to 8 servings

Ingredients
2 pork tenderloins cut in half, then in quarters lengthwise (you should have 16 pieces)
2 tablespoons olive oil
2 tablespoons Spice Delight BBQ Rub
1 cup Spice Delight Sweet & Zesty BBQ Sauce

Method
1. Rub pork tenderloins all over with olive oil. Sprinkle evenly with Spice Delight BBQ Rub.
2. Let marinate in refrigerator for 1 hour.
3. Heat a grill pan over high heat.
4. When hot, place tenderloins in pan. Do no crown pan. Work in batches if necessary. After 5 minutes brush with BBQ sauce and turn. Repeat until pieces are cooked through.

Tips
● You can cook that on an outdoor grill. Be sure to watch pieces carefully. Turn and brush with sauce often to avoid burning. Increase time as needed to insure tenderloins are done. Check with thermometer to make sure internal temperature is 160 degrees.
● Discard basting sauce and use fresh sauce if you need more sauce at serving time.

BBQ Meatloaf

This meatloaf is flavored with my Spice Delight BBQ Rub and Sweet & Zesty BBQ Sauce.

Makes 4 to 6 servings

Ingredients
1 lb. ground beef chuck or ground turkey
1 cup breadcrumbs
2 large eggs, beaten
½ cup Spice Delight Sweet & Zesty BBQ Sauce
2 tablespoons Spice Delight BBQ Rub
½ cup medium onion, diced small
½ cup green bell pepper, diced small

Method
1. Preheat oven to 350 degrees.
2. Combine all ingredients in a large bowl.
3. Mix well so that all ingredients are blended.
4. Press mixture evenly in a 9-inch loaf pan.
5. Bake 1 hour. Slice and serve with extra BBQ sauce if desired.

Notes:

Chapter 5:
Sauces & Condiments

This chapter contains recipes for dressings, dips and delicious chunky chutneys. They can be paired with main dishes, drizzled on salads and fruit or spread on burgers. These recipes are simple to make and you can keep them in the refrigerator for use anytime. By making your own condiments you control sugar, fat and salt content. What could be better than that?

Chapter 5:
Sauces & Condiments

Curry Sauce

Makes 4 servings

Ingredients
2 tablespoons canola oil
¼ cup red onion, diced small
¼ cup green bell pepper, diced small
½ teaspoon curry powder
½ teaspoon dried thyme leaves
1 tablespoon Spice Delight All-Purpose Essence
2 tablespoons flour
2 cups low-sodium chicken stock

Method
1. Heat oil in a medium size saucepan over medium heat.
2. Add onion, bell pepper, curry powder, thyme and Spice Delight All-Purpose Essence.
3. Sauté 5 minutes or until vegetables are tender.
4. Stir flour into vegetables; cook 3 minutes stirring constantly.
5. Add a little chicken stock; stir until flour is smooth.
6. Add remainder stock; simmer 10 minutes until sauce thickens.

Pepper Mushroom & Onion Glaze

This makes a great topping for any meat.

Makes 4 servings

Ingredients
1 tablespoon olive oil
¼ cup green bell pepper, diced small
¼ cup red onion, diced small
¼ cup button mushrooms, sliced thin
1 teaspoon dried basil leaves
1 tablespoon Spice Delight All-Purpose Essence
2 cups low-sodium chicken stock
3 tablespoons cornstarch
2 tablespoons water

Method
1. Heat oil in medium size saucepan over medium heat.
2. Add bell pepper, onion, mushrooms, basil and Spice Delight All-Purpose Essence. Cook 3 minutes.
3. Add chicken stock; bring to boil.
4. Dissolve cornstarch in water.
5. Pour cornstarch mix into sauce while stirring.
6. Stop pouring when you reach your desired thickness.

Tricolor Peppercorn Glaze

The bold flavor or this glaze works well with beef.

Makes 4 to 6 servings

Ingredients

1 tablespoon vegetable oil
1 tablespoon minced shallots
1 teaspoon dried thyme leaves
1 teaspoon tricolor peppercorn, cracked
1 tablespoon Spice Delight All-Purpose Essence
2 cups low-sodium beef stock
¼ cup red wine (your favorite)
3 tablespoons cornstarch
2 tablespoons water

Method

1. In a medium size saucepan over medium heat, sauté the first 5 ingredients; cook 3 minutes.
2. Add beef stock and wine; bring to a slight simmer.
3. Dissolve cornstarch in water.
4. Pour cornstarch mixture into sauce while stirring.
5. Stop pouring when you reach your desired thickness.

Mustard-Peppercorn Glaze

Makes 6 to 8 servings

Ingredients

1 cup chicken stock
1 cup beef stock
1 teaspoon dry rosemary
1 teaspoon Spice Delight All-Purpose Essence
1 tablespoon prepared mustard
1 teaspoon cracked black pepper
2 tablespoons cornstarch
2 tablespoons water

Method

1. In a medium size saucepan over medium heat, add the first 6 ingredients listed above.
2. Bring glaze to a slight boil.
3. Dissolve cornstarch in water.
4. Pour cornstarch mixture into sauce while stirring.
5. Stop pouring when you reach your desired thickness.

Spicy Chipotle Mayo

Makes 8 to 10 servings

Ingredients
2 cups Hellmann's canola oil mayonnaise
1 chipotle pepper in adobo sauce, minced
¼ teaspoon chili powder
1 teaspoon fresh squeezed lime juice
2 teaspoons chopped flat leaf parsley

Method
1. Whisk all ingredients together in medium size bowl.
2. Store in refrigerator.

Tip
Use as a dipping sauce or spread for sandwiches or burgers.

Toast Points with Cinnamon-Apple Chutney

Makes 2 to 4 servings

Ingredients
2 slices multi-grain bread
2 teaspoons Smart Balance Butter Substitute
2 Granny Smith apples, peeled, cored, diced medium
¼ cup dark raisins
1 tablespoon raw brown sugar
½ teaspoon ground cinnamon
1 tablespoon finely chopped pecans

Method
1. Toast bread; set aside.
2. Preheat pan a few minutes over medium heat. Melt butter substitute in pan.
3. Add apples, raisins, brown sugar and cinnamon. Sauté until apples are tender, 8 to 10 minutes.
4. Once apples are tender, slice toast twice diagonally to create four triangles.
5. Top toast points with chutney.
6. Garnish toast points with pecans.

Pineapple-Peach Chutney

This chutney is light and refreshing and goes well with fish and chicken.

Makes 4 to 6 servings

Ingredients
2 tablespoons canola oil
1 tablespoon shallot, finely chopped
1 cup peaches, diced medium
1 tablespoon grated fresh ginger
1 teaspoon cider vinegar
1 fresh pineapple, peeled, cored, diced medium
¼ cup light brown sugar or turbinado sugar (sugar in the raw)

Method
1. In a large stockpot over medium heat, sauté shallot in oil for 3 minutes.
2. Add peaches and ginger; sauté for another 2 minutes.
3. Stir in vinegar, pineapple and sugar. Cook 20 minutes over low heat, stirring occasionally.

Dried Plums with Ancho Chili

Most know about prunes, which are now referred to as dried plums. They add great sweetness to this unique flavorful sauce.

Makes 2 to 4 servings

Ingredients

1 teaspoon Smart Balance Butter Substitute
4 large ancho chilies
½ white onion, chopped medium
½ cup chopped fresh tomato
½ lb. pitted dried plums (prunes)
1 teaspoon Spice Delight All-Purpose Essence
2 cups chicken stock (Better Than Bouillon Brand)
½ cup orange juice
1 tablespoon cornstarch
1 tablespoon water

Method

1. In a large stockpot add first 8 ingredients; cook 20 minutes over medium heat.
2. Let cool. Blend in blender or food processor until smooth.
3. Pour blended sauce into medium saucepan over medium heat.
4. Dissolve cornstarch in water.
5. Pour cornstarch mixture into sauce while stirring.
6. Stop pouring when you reach your desired thickness.
7. Let simmer for 3 minutes.

Spice Delight's Collection

Comfort Foods
of the South

Chef Barry Moody

Parmesan Turkey Burger
p. 83

**Omelet Burrito Wrap
with Salsa
p. 60**

Grilled NY Strip Steak with Onions and Mushrooms
p. 69

BBQ Hawaiian Chicken
p. 88

Chicken Sausage Hoagie
p. 82

Mustard-Rosemary Lamb Tenderloin
p. 84

Succotash Rice
p. 50

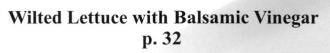

Wilted Lettuce with Balsamic Vinegar
p. 32

Grilled Eggplant Napoleons
p.151

Angel Hair Pasta with Tofu & Basil
p. 150

**White Bean Soup with
Kale & Tomatoes
p. 19**

Spicy Shrimp with Penne Pasta
p. 139

Pan-Fried Lobster Burger
p. 145

Grilled Tuna with Tomato-Basil Salsa
p. 146

Seafood Chowder
p. 23

BBQ Salmon
p. 94

Sorrell Ginger Drink
p. 168

Orange Bellini
p. 171

Pineapple Rice with Raisins & Pecans
p. 53

Pan-Fried Peaches with Pound Cake & Ice Cream
p. 188

Nutella & Banana Sandwich
p. 192

Banana Chocolate Shakes
p. 175

Rice Pudding
p. 191

Asian BBQ Sauce

This Asian BBQ Sauce will give you something new to add to your ribs, chicken or steak.

Makes 2 o 4 servings

Ingredients
¼ cup hoisin sauce
1 chipotle pepper in adobo sauce, minced
2 tablespoons soy sauce
½ cup white wine
½ cup light brown sugar
¼ teaspoon sesame oil

Method
1. Place hoisin sauce, chipotle pepper, soy sauce, wine, brown sugar and sesame oil in a medium size sauccpan; mix well.
2. Turn heat to low; simmer 20 minutes stirring occasionally.

Tip
Hoisin sauce, also called Chinese barbecue sauce, is frequently used in Asian stir-fries and marinades. Made from a combination of fermented soy, garlic, vinegar, and usually chilies and sweetener, hoisin is dark in color and thick in consistency. You can find it in the Asian section of the grocery store.

Roasted Red Pepper Vinaigrette

Makes 2 to 4 servings

Ingredients

1 red bell pepper, roasted
1 garlic clove, roasted
2 tablespoons balsamic vinegar
1 teaspoon Spice Delight All-Purpose Essence
½ cup olive oil

Method

1. Roast bell pepper and garlic (see instructions below).
2. Place pepper, garlic, vinegar, Spice Delight All-Purpose Essence and olive oil in a blender or food processor. Purée until smooth.
3. Slowly pour in olive oil while the motor is running.

Tips

● To roast pepper, place directly on burner of stove over medium high heat or in a 500 degree oven on a sheet pan. Char all over; then place in paper bag or in a bowl covered with plastic wrap until cool enough to handle. Peel skin off peppers. Cut open and remove and discard seeds and ribs.
● To roast garlic, cut the top off a whole head of garlic. Pour 1 teaspoon olive oil over the top. Place on a cookie sheet pan. Roast in a 500 degree oven for 20 minutes or until tender. When cool enough to handle remove one bulb and squeeze out pulp.
● You can purchase roasted garlic and peppers from the salad bar to make this vinaigrette.

Mango Chutney

This Indian chutney goes well with Curried Chicken and Rice Pilaf.

Makes 4 servings

Ingredients
2 cups diced mango, fresh or frozen
1 cup apple juice
½ cup chopped dried apricots
½ teaspoon Spice Delight BBQ Rub
2 teaspoons apple cider vinegar

Method
1. In a large stockpot mix together mango, apple juice and dried apricots. Bring mixture to a simmer.
2. Stir in Spice Delight BBQ Rub and vinegar.
3. Cook chutney 25 minutes, stirring occasionally to avoid burning.
4. Place in a serving bowl. Serve at room temperature or chilled.

Mango Salsa

This refreshing salsa is especially nice with chicken, seafood or pork.

Makes 2 to 4 servings

Ingredients

1 ripe fresh mango, diced small
2 tablespoons red onion, diced small
2 tablespoons green bell pepper, diced small
Juice of 1 lime
1 teaspoon clover honey
1 teaspoon cider vinegar
1 teaspoon Spice Delight All-Purpose Essence

Method

1. In a medium bowl, mix together mango, onion and pepper; set aside.
2. Whisk together remaining ingredients.
3. Pour lime juice mixture over fruit mixture. Toss to coat.
4. Chill salsa until serving time.

Vegetarian Portabella Cream Sauce

Portabella mushrooms are large and meaty. They make a wonderful addition to any dish. They are actually the grown-up version of a brown Cremini mushroom and will do nicely if you can't find Portabellas.

Makes 4 servings

Ingredients
2 tablespoons olive oil, divided
1 cup Portabella mushrooms, sliced thin
2 tablespoons red onion, diced small
⅓ cup all-purpose flour
3 cups vegetable stock (Better Than Bouillon brand)
2 teaspoons Spice Delight All-Purpose Essence
¼ cup low-fat half & half

Method
1. Heat 1 tablespoon olive oil in a medium size sauté pan over medium heat.
2. Add mushrooms, Spice Delight All-Purpose Essence and onion; sauté 4 minutes or until tender.
3. Remove veggies from pan; set aside.
4. Add flour and remaining tablespoon oil; whisk until flour blends with oil.
5. Add ½ cup vegetable stock while whisking until sauce is smooth.
6. Add remainder stock and whisk constantly to prevent lumps.
7. Return vegetables to sauce; stir in half & half. Simmer 15 minutes.

Zesty Ranch Dipping Sauce

This makes a nice dipping sauce for chicken wings, nuggets and fries.

Makes 4 to 6 servings

Ingredients
1 ½ cups low-fat ranch dressing
2 tablespoons ketchup
A dash Texas Pete Hot Sauce or to taste

Method
1. Whisk together all ingredients listed above.
2. Pour into a serving bowl.
3. Cover and chill before serving.

Sherry-Mustard Vinaigrette

Serve this vinaigrette over roasted vegetables, salads or grilled chicken and fish.

Makes 2 to 4 servings

Ingredients
¼ cup sherry vinegar
1 tablespoon whole grain mustard
1 teaspoon fresh tarragon, chopped fine
¼ cup extra virgin olive oil
1 teaspoon Spice Delight All-Purpose Essence

Method
1. Place all ingredients listed above in a blender container. Blend for 30 seconds.
2. Pour into a serving bowl. Cover and chill until serving time.

BBQ Sauce

This BBQ sauce is somewhat like my Spice Delight Sweet & Zesty BBQ Sauce. It can be used in any recipe that calls for BBQ sauce. It's delicious!

Makes 6 to 8 servings

Ingredients
2 cups ketchup
1 cup spring water
¼ cup cider vinegar
¼ cup dark brown sugar
1 teaspoon Spice Delight All-Purpose Essence
1 teaspoon hickory liquid smoke
½ teaspoon chili powder
½ teaspoon garlic powder

Method
1. In a medium saucepan, combine all ingredients listed above; mix well.
2. Heat sauce over medium heat to a gentle simmer.
3. Cook over low heat for 1 hour. Stir every 15 minutes to make sure that sauce does not stick or burn.

Tip
If you want a little heat, add a pinch of crushed red pepper flakes or a dash of hot sauce.

Notes:

Chapter 6: Wontons

Wontons are a noodle-dough dumpling typically filled with spiced minced pork or other ground meat or vegetables. These little pockets of flavor can be filled with just about anything you can come up with. You can find wonton wrappers in the produce section of your grocery store or order them online. I have dedicated an entire chapter to them because they offer such a huge opportunity for creative, quick and easy cooking. I couldn't resist sharing my ideas for fillings. They are easy to make if you follow my method.

1. Mince or dice your filling.
2. To assemble, just mound 1 tablespoon of filling in the center of wonton wrap.
3. Next, wet edges of the wonton wrapper; top with another wonton wrapper.
4. To insure that the wontons will not come apart during the cooking process; press the edges of filled wontons firmly with a fork. At the same time, press out the air around the filling.
5. In a large 6-quart pot, bring salted water to a boil. Then lower to a simmer.
6. Carefully place wontons in simmering water. Cook for about 6 minutes, until wontons rise to the surface. Avoid boiling the water vigorously after you add the wontons because this will cause the wontons to break apart. Remove wontons with a slotted spoon and place on a greased or buttered sheet pan while cooking the rest of the wontons.

Tips
- When making wontons, put a little flour on the surface where you are working.
- Also, keep the wonton wrappers in plastic wrap until you are ready to use in order to keep them from dryng out.

Chapter 6:
Wontons

Ricotta and Parmesan Wontons

This is a simple way to make cheese ravioli.

Makes 15 wontons

Ingredients
1 lb. low-sodium Ricotta cheese
¼ cup low-sodium Parmesan cheese
2 tablespoons fresh basil, chopped fine
2 teaspoons Spice Delight All-Purpose Essence
30 wonton wrappers, thawed

Method
1. In a medium size bowl combine cheeses, herbs and Spice Delight All-Purpose Essence.
2. To assemble, mound 1 tablespoon filling in the middle of wonton wrap.
3. Next, wet the edges of wonton and top with another wonton wrap.
4. To insure that the wontons will not come apart during the cooking process; press the edges of wontons firmly with a fork. At the same time, press out the air around the filling.
5. In a large 6-quart pot, bring salted water to a boil. Then lower to a simmer.
6. Carefully place wontons in simmering water. Cook for about 6 minutes, until wontons rise to the surface. Avoid boiling the water vigorously after you add wontons because this will cause wontons to break apart. Remove with slotted spoon and place on a greased or buttered sheet pan while cooking the rest of wontons.

Curry Shrimp Wontons

Makes 15 wontons

Ingredients
2 tablespoons green bell pepper, chopped fine
2 tablespoons red onion, chopped fine
½ teaspoon dried thyme leaves
½ teaspoon curry powder
2 teaspoons Spice Delight All-Purpose Essence
1 teaspoon vegetable oil
1 lb. raw shrimp, peeled, deveined, chopped small
30 wonton wrappers, thawed

Method
1. In a food processor or blender, pulse the bell pepper, onion, thyme, curry powder and Spice Delight All-Purpose Essence.
2. In a medium size pot over medium high heat, sauté vegetables for 4 minutes in vegetable oil. Add shrimp. Cook until shrimp turns pink and opaque.
3. Let cool.
4. To assemble, mound 1 tablespoon filling in the middle of wonton wrap.
5. Next, wet the edges of wonton and top with another wonton wrap.
6. To insure that the wontons will not come apart during the cooking process; press the edges of wontons firmly with a fork. At the same time, press out the air around the filling.
7. In a large 6-quart pot, bring salted water to a boil. Then lower to a simmer.
8. Carefully place wontons in simmering water. Cook for about 6 minutes, until wontons rise to the surface. Avoid boiling the water vigorously after you add wontons because this will cause wontons to break apart. Remove with slotted spoon and place on a greased or buttered sheet pan while cooking the rest of wontons.

Chicken and Portabella Mushroom Wontons

Makes 15 wontons

Ingredients
1 lb. rotisserie chicken, pulled off the bone
½ cup Portabella mushrooms, chopped fine
2 teaspoons Spice Delight All-Purpose Essence
2 tablespoons scallions, diced small
1 tablespoon vegetable oil
30 wonton wrappers, thawed

Method
1. In a food processor or blender, pulse chicken, mushrooms, scallions and Spice Delight All-Purpose Essence.
2. In a medium size saucepan over medium high heat, sauté mixture for 4 minutes in vegetable oil.
3. To assemble, mound 1 tablespoon filling in the middle of wonton wrap.
4. Next, wet the edges of wonton and top with another wonton wrap.
5. To insure that the wontons will not come apart during the cooking process; press the edges of wontons firmly with a fork. At the same time, press out the air around the filling.
6. In a large 6-quart pot, bring salted water to a boil. Then lower to a simmer.
7. Carefully place wontons in simmering water. Cook for about 6 minutes, until wontons rise to the surface. Avoid boiling the water vigorously after you add wontons because this will cause wontons to break apart. Remove with slotted spoon and place on a greased or buttered sheet pan while cooking the rest of wontons.

Spicy Ground Pork Wontons

Makes 15 wontons

Ingredients
1 lb. ground pork
2 tablespoons Spice Delight All-Purpose Essence
¼ cup scallions, diced small
1 tablespoon vegetable oil
30 wonton wrappers, thawed

Method
1. In a food processor or blender, pulse ground pork, Spice Delight All-Purpose Essence and scallions.
2. In a medium size saucepan over medium high heat, sauté mixture for 4 minutes in vegetable oil until there is no pink.
3. To assemble, mound 1 tablespoon filling in the middle of wonton wrap.
4. Next, wet the edges of wonton and top with another wonton wrap.
5. To insure that the wontons will not come apart during the cooking process; press the edges of wontons firmly with a fork. At the same time, press out the air around the filling.
6. In a large 6-quart pot, bring salted water to a boil. Then lower to a simmer.
7. Carefully place wontons in simmering water. Cook for about 6 minutes, until wontons rise to the surface. Avoid boiling the water vigorously after you add wontons because this will cause wontons to break apart. Remove with slotted spoon and place on a greased or buttered sheet pan while cooking the rest of wontons.

Salmon with Lemon and Dill Wontons

Makes 15 wontons

Ingredients

2 cups clam or chicken stock
Juice of 1 lemon
1 lb. salmon filet, poached with skin removed or 1 can of salmon
2 tablespoons dried dill weed
2 teaspoons Spice Delight All-Purpose Essence
30 wonton wrappers, thawed

Method

1. Bring clam juice and lemon juice to a boil in a medium size saucepan over medium heat. Reduce heat; lower to a simmer. Carefully add salmon. Cook 5 minutes until salmon is cooked through. If using canned salmon, drain salmon; remove bones.
2. In a food processor or blender, pulse salmon, dill weed and Spice Delight All-Purpose Essence.
3. To assemble, mound 1 tablespoon filling in the middle of wonton wrap.
4. Next, wet the edges of wonton and top with another wonton wrap.
5. To insure that the wontons will not come apart during the cooking process; press the edges of wontons firmly with a fork. At the same time, press out the air around the filling.
6. In a large 6-quart pot, bring salted water to a boil. Then lower to a simmer.
7. Carefully place wontons in simmering water. Cook for about 6 minutes, until wontons rise to the surface. Avoid boiling the water vigorously after you add wontons because this will cause wontons to break apart. Remove with slotted spoon and place on a greased or buttered sheet pan while cooking the rest of wontons.

Sweet Potato Wontons

Makes 15 wontons

Ingredients

1 lb. sweet potatoes, mashed (you can use canned sweet potatoes)
2 teaspoons brown sugar
2 tablespoons Spice Delight BBQ Rub
1 teaspoon ground cinnamon
1 teaspoon sea salt
30 wonton wrappers, thawed

Method

1. In a medium size bowl, mix together all the ingredients listed above except wonton wrappers.
2. To assemble, mound 1 tablespoon filling in the middle of wonton wrap.
3. Next, wet the edges of wonton and top with another wonton wrap.
4. To insure that the wontons will not come apart during the cooking process; press the edges of wontons firmly with a fork. At the same time, press out the air around the filling.
5. In a large 6-quart pot, bring salted water to a boil. Then lower to a simmer.
6. Carefully place wontons in simmering water. Cook for about 6 minutes, until wontons rise to the surface. Avoid boiling the water vigorously after you add wontons because this will cause wontons to break apart. Remove with slotted spoon and place on a greased or buttered sheet pan while cooking the rest of wontons.

Potatoes with Peas & Cheddar Wontons

This wonton reminds me of Samosas, the fried appetizer that I once ate at the Indian stores in New York City. I've eliminated the frying to create a healthier version with the same great flavor.

Makes 15 wontons

Ingredients
2 cups mashed potatoes, cooled
¼ cup green peas (thawed)
3 tablespoons low-fat Cheddar cheese
2 teaspoons Spice Delight All-Purpose Essence
1 teaspoon dried thyme leaves
1 teaspoon curry powder
30 wonton wrappers, thawed

Method
1. In a mixing bowl, mix together all ingredients listed above except wonton wrappers.
2. To assemble, mound 1 tablespoon filling in the middle of wonton wrap.
3. Next, wet the edges of wonton and top with another wonton wrap.
4. To insure that the wontons will not come apart during the cooking process; press the edges of wontons firmly with a fork. At the same time, press out the air around the filling.
5. In a large 6-quart pot, bring salted water to a boil. Then lower to a simmer.
6. Carefully place wontons in simmering water. Cook for about 6 minutes, until wontons rise to the surface. Avoid boiling the water vigorously after you add wontons because this will cause wontons to break apart. Remove with slotted spoon and place on a greased or buttered sheet pan while cooking the rest of wontons.

Notes:

Chapter 7:
Seafood

Seafood is an important part of a well-balanced, nutritious diet. Fish and shellfish are incredibly quick-cooking and accept seasonings and flavorings well. Certain types of fish are delicate and others are sturdy. This will determine the best cooking and seasoning methods. Perfectly cooked fish is moist and opaque in color and flakes easily. Fish is a good source of protein and it's not high in saturated fat. Whether you eat fresh fish, canned fish or frozen fish, you should keep it on hand for quick and easy meals. Salmon is a fish that's a good source of omega-3 fatty acids. Omega-3 fatty acids benefit the hearts of healthy people and those that are at high risk of, or who have, cardiovascular disease. Start your children to eating fish when they are young and they will reap the benefits well into adulthood. Serve with fresh vegetables and salads for a well-balanced meal.

Chapter 7:
Seafood

Parmesan Panko Crusted Tilapia

Makes 3 to 4 servings

Ingredients
1 cup Panko breadcrumbs
1 tablespoon Parmesan cheese
3 teaspoons Spice Delight All-Purpose Essence, divided
1 tablespoon olive oil
1 lb. Tilapia fillets

Method
1. Preheat oven to 350 degrees.
2. In a shallow dish mix breadcrumbs, Parmesan and 2 teaspoons Spice Delight All-Purpose Essence; set aside.
3. Rub oil evenly over Tilapia; dust both sides with remaining 1 teaspoon Spice Delight All-Purpose Essence.
4. Dredge Tilapia in breadcrumb mixture to coat both sides.
5. Place fish on an oiled rimmed cookie sheet. Bake 20 minutes or until fish is flaky.

Herb Baked Scallops

Scallops are so tender they just melt in your mouth. The large sea scallops are sweet and satisfying.

Makes 4 servings

Ingredients
8 large sea scallops
1 tablespoon olive oil
2 teaspoons Spice Delight All-Purpose Essence
1 cup seasoned breadcrumbs
½ teaspoon dried basil leaves
1 sheet parchment paper

Method
1. Preheat oven to 350 degrees prior to baking.
2. Place scallops in a bowl, toss with olive oil. Sprinkle with Spice Delight All-Purpose Essence. Cover and refrigerate 30 minutes.
3. Mix breadcrumbs with basil.
4. Dredge scallops in breadcrumb mixture to coat all sides.
5. Place scallops on a rimmed cookie sheet lined with parchment paper.
6. Bake 15 to 18 minutes.

Poached Halibut with Ginger & Curry

Poaching seafood with flavorful stocks imparts great flavor. It is a very simple French method for cooking fish.

Makes 2 to 4 servings

Ingredients
1 teaspoon olive oil
½ cup red onion, diced medium
2 cups clam or chicken stock
1 cup baby carrots
1 tablespoon Spice Delight All-Purpose Essence
1 teaspoon curry powder
1 teaspoon fresh ginger, peeled and minced
1 lb. Halibut fillets

Method
1. In a large saucepan, heat oil over medium heat.
2. Sauté onion 3 to 5 minutes.
3. Add clam or chicken stock, carrots, Spice Delight All-Purpose Essence and curry powder. Bring to a boil. Reduce heat to low and bring liquid to barely a simmer.
4. Add Halibut; cook 5 to 8 minutes or until Halibut is opaque and flakes easily.

Tip
When you add Halibut to stock, cover with lid to prevent loss of stock.

Corn Meal Crusted Tilapia

Corn meal gives the Tilapia a nice crunchy texture. Fine corn meal is the best for this recipe.

Makes 3 to 4 servings

Ingredients
3 large egg whites
2 tablespoons water
2 teaspoons Spice Delight All-Purpose Essence
1 lb. Tilapia fillets
1 cup fine corn meal
2 tablespoons olive oil

Method
1. In a medium size bowl, mix egg whites, water and 1 teaspoon Spice Delight All-Purpose Essence.
2. Coat both sides of fish with egg mixture.
3. Combine corn meal with remaining Spice Delight All-Purpose Essence.
4. Coat both sides of fish with corn meal mixture.
5. Heat oil in large skillet over medium heat.
6. Sauté fish 3 ½ minutes per side until golden and crispy.

Salmon Dill Burgers

Salmon burgers are a great way to eat Salmon. Make sure to ask your butcher to remove the skin from the fillets.

Makes 4 servings

Ingredients
1 lb. wild Salmon fillets
1 tablespoon fresh chopped dill weed
1 teaspoon black pepper, coarsely ground
Juice of 1 lime
2 tablespoons Spice Delight All-Purpose Essence
2 cups Panko breadcrumbs
3 tablespoons olive oil

Method
1. Place Salmon, dill, black pepper and lime juice in food processor bowl.
2. Pulse mixture a few times until Salmon is minced.
3. Place Salmon in a bowl and mix by hand until spices are evenly blended.
4. Form into 4 flat burgers; dust both sides evenly with Spice Delight All-Purpose Essence. Cover and refrigerate 30 minutes.
5. Dredge both sides in Panko breadcrumbs.
6. Pan-fry in oil over medium heat 3 to 5 minutes per side or until golden brown.

Spicy Shrimp with Penne Pasta

This recipe is dedicated to Stephanie M. It's one of my favorite pasta meals.

Makes 4 to 6 servings

Ingredients
2 tablespoons olive oil
2 tablespoons red onion, diced medium
2 tablespoons green bell peppers, diced medium
2 tablespoons button mushrooms, sliced thin
1 tablespoon Spice Delight All-Purpose Essence
1 teaspoon dried basil leaves
2 lbs. shrimp, peeled and deveined
2 teaspoons blackened seasoning
1 package (8 oz.) Penne pasta, cooked
½ cup low-sodium chicken stock
1 tablespoon salted butter
½ cup Roma tomatoes, diced medium

Method
1. Heat olive oil in a large stockpot over medium heat.
2. Add onion, bell pepper, mushrooms, Spice Delight All-Purpose Essence and basil; cook for 3 minutes.
3. Toss shrimp with blackened seasoning.
4. Add shrimp to stockpot; cook 2 minutes.
5. Sir in cooked pasta, chicken stock and butter.
6. Cook 2 minutes longer or until heated through.
7. Turn off heat; stir in tomatoes.

Tip
You can top this pasta with fresh grated Parmesan cheese and chopped fresh basil, if desired.

Peppercorn-Lime Salmon Burgers

This burger has bold flavor from the tricolor peppercorns and lime juice. It will give you that Key West vibe.

Makes 4 servings

Ingredients
1 lb. wild Salmon fillets (skin removed)
2 tablespoons tricolor peppercorns, crushed fine
Juice of 1 lime
2 teaspoons Spice Delight All-Purpose Essence
2 cups Panko breadcrumbs
2 tablespoons olive oil

Method
1. Place Salmon, peppercorns and lime juice in food processor.
2. Pulse mixture a few times until Salmon is minced.
3. Place in a bowl and mix by hand until spices are evenly blended.
4. Form into 4 flat Salmon burgers; dust both sides with Spice Delight All-Purpose Essence. Cover and refrigerate 30 minutes.
5. Dredge both sides of burgers in Panko breadcrumbs.
6. Pan-fry in oil over medium heat 3 to 5 minutes per side or until golden brown.

Salmon Burgers with BBQ Rub

The sweet and spicy burger will make your mouth jump for joy!

Makes 4 servings

Ingredients
1lb. wild Salmon fillets (skin removed)
2 teaspoons fresh lemon juice
2 tablespoons Spice Delight BBQ Rub
1 teaspoon dried thyme leaves
2 tablespoons olive oil
2 cups Panko breadcrumbs

Method
1. Place Salmon, lemon juice, Spice Delight BBQ Rub and thyme in food processor.
2. Pulse mixture a few times until Salmon is minced.
3. Place in a bowl and mix by hand until spices are evenly blended.
4. Form into 4 flat Salmon burgers; cover and refrigerate 30 minutes.
5. Dredge both sides of burgers in Panko breadcrumbs.
6. Pan-fry in oil over medium heat 3 to 5 minutes per side or until golden brown.

Pan-Fried Halibut

I love this mild, flaky fish. It can take the strong flavors of the seasonings.

Makes 3 to 4 servings

Ingredients
1 tablespoon Spice Delight All-Purpose Essence
½ teaspoon dried thyme leaves
1 teaspoon Cajun spice or blackening spice
1 lb. Halibut
2 tablespoons olive oil

Method
1. Mix Spice Delight All-Purpose Essence, thyme and Cajun or blackening spice in a small bowl.
2. Rub olive oil on both sides of Halibut.
3. Dust an even coating of spice mix on both sides. Save remainder of spice mix in a zip lock bag for future use.
4. Cover and refrigerate 30 minutes.
5. Heat oil in medium size skillet over medium heat.
6. Sauté Halibut 3 minutes per side or until fish is flaky.

Pan-Fried Grouper with Capers & Parmesan Cheese

Makes 3 to 4 servings

Ingredients

1 lb. Grouper fillets
1 teaspoon Spice Delight All-Purpose Essence
1 tablespoon olive oil
½ cup white wine
1 teaspoon capers (drained)
½ cup fresh grated Parmesan cheese
2 tablespoons chopped sun-dried tomatoes

Method

1. Dust both sides of Grouper with Spice Delight All-Purpose Essence. Cover and marinate in refrigerator 30 minutes.
2. Preheat broiler.
3. Heat oil in a large oven-proof skillet over medium heat. Sauté fish 3 minutes per side. Remove fish from pan; set aside.
4. Add wine and capers to skillet and cook for 1 minute, scraping up any brown bits in bottom of pan.
5. Return fish to skillet. Top with Parmesan cheese.
6. Broil 3 minutes or until golden brown.
7. Garnish with tomatoes. Serve in a bowl.

Grouper with Capers & Tomatoes

Makes 4 servings

Ingredients
1 teaspoon olive oil
½ cup red onion, diced small
½ cup green bell pepper, diced small
1 teaspoon dried basil leaves *or* 1 tablespoon chopped fresh basil
1 (28 oz.) can whole plum tomatoes, drained, chopped medium
1 tablespoon capers, drained
1 teaspoon Better that Bouillon Chicken Base
1 teaspoon Spice Delight All-Purpose Essence
1 lb. Grouper or Tuna fillets

Method
1. Heat oil in a large skillet over medium heat.
2. Sauté onion, bell pepper and basil in oil 4 minutes or until vegetables are tender.
3. Stir in tomatoes, capers and chicken base. Lower heat and simmer 10 minutes or until most of liquid has reduced; set aside.
4. Rub fish on both sides with olive oil.
5. Dust both sides of fish with an even amount of Spice Delight All-Purpose Essence.
6. Heat oil in sauté pan or grill pan. Cook fish 4 minutes per side or until flaky.
7. Place fish on a serving platter and pour sauce over top.

Tip
Start with fish no more than ½-inch thick.

Pan-Fried Lobster Burger

This is simply for the seafood lover in you. Move over crab cakes!

Makes 2 servings

Ingredients

1 cooked Lobster tail
2 tablespoons vegetable oil, divided
1 tablespoon green bell pepper, diced small
1 tablespoon red onion, diced small
1 teaspoon celery, diced small
1 tablespoon Spice Delight All-Purpose Essence
1 tablespoon Hellmann's mayonnaise
1 tablespoon dried thyme leaves
1 cup plus 2 tablespoons breadcrumbs, divided

Method

1. Dice Lobster and place in a large bowl; set aside.
2. Heat oil in large skillet over medium heat.
3. Sauté bell pepper, onion and celery with Spice Delight All-Purpose Essence for 5 minutes. Add to Lobster in bowl; let mixture cool.
4. Add 2 tablespoons breadcrumbs and mayonnaise to the Lobster mixture; gently fold until combined.
5. Make 2 or 4 flat patties; bread both sides with remaining 1 cup breadcrumbs.
6. Heat remaining oil in skillet over medium heat. Pan-fry 3 minutes per side or until golden brown.

Grilled Tuna with Tomato-Basil Salsa

This grilled tuna topped with a light and colorful salsa is simple to make and refreshing to eat.

Makes 2 servings

Ingredients
2 (6 oz.) Tuna steaks
1 tablespoon olive oil
2 teaspoons Spice Delight All-Purpose Essence
1 teaspoon dried basil leaves
Tomato-Basil Salsa
2 large tomatoes, diced small
2 tablespoons red onion, diced
1 tablespoon olive oil
2 tablespoons balsamic vinegar
2 teaspoons Spice Delight All-Purpose Essence
1 to 2 tablespoons fresh basil, minced
1 tablespoon capers, drained

Method
1. Rub olive oil on both sides of Tuna steaks.
2. Combine Spice Delight All-Purpose Essence and basil.
3. Dust spice mixture evenly on both sides of Tuna.
4. Cover and refrigerate 1 hour.
5. Grill over medium high heat 3 minutes per side. Cover with foil to keep warm until serving time.
6. To make Tomato-Basil Salsa, combine all ingredients in a medium sized bowl.
7. Cover and let sit at room temperature until ready to serve.
8. To serve, spoon salsa over grilled Tuna.

Notes:

Chapter 8:
Vegetarian

We can also get protein from many other foods besides meats. Try the recipes in this chapter and learn to cook some of the meat alternatives that are available. Try to cook vegetarian once or twice a week. Eating healthy is not about denial; it's about making moderations in the choices we make.

Chapter 8:
Vegetarian

Angel Hair Pasta with Tofu & Basil

This vegetarian meal is light and refreshing as a main entrée served with a green salad and crusty bread.

Makes 2 to 4 servings

Ingredients

2 cups angel hair pasta, cooked according to package directions
½ cup extra firm tofu
2 teaspoons Spice Delight All-Purpose Essence, divided
2 tablespoons extra virgin olive oil
1 tablespoon fresh basil leaves, finely chopped
½ cup grape tomatoes, cut in half

Method

1. Place hot pasta in a large serving bowl. Toss with 1 teaspoon Spice Delight All-Purpose Essence.
2. Drain tofu; dice into ½-inch pieces. Toss with remaining Spice Delight All-Purpose Essence. Add to the bowl with pasta.
3. Add olive oil, basil and grape tomatoes. Toss together and serve immediately.

Tip

Here's an option to add more flavor and color. Add 1 to 2 tablespoons capers or chopped olives at step 3. Top finished pasta with freshly grated Parmesan cheese.

Grilled Eggplant Napoleons

Eggplants are a beautiful, tasty and very nutritious vegetable.

Makes 2 to 4 servings

Ingredients
2 medium size eggplants, sliced into ½-inch rounds (you will need at least
    12 rounds for a 3 layer napoleon)
2 tablespoons olive oil
2 tablespoons Spice Delight All-Purpose Essence
1 tablespoon dried Italian seasoning
8 (¼-inch) thick slices Mozzarella cheese
8 (½-inch) thick tomato slices from 2 large tomatoes
¼ cup Italian dressing (your favorite)

Method
1. Heat gas grill to medium high (approximately 350 to 355 degrees) or
   if using a grill pan on a stovetop, heat over high heat until very hot,
   but not smoking.
2. Brush both sides of eggplant slices with olive oil to prevent sticking.
   Mix together Spice Delight All-Purpose Essence and Italian seasoning.
   Sprinkle both sides if eggplant with spicc mixture. Let rest a minute.
   Grill eggplant for 5 to 7 minutes per side until lightly charred and
   tender.
3. Assemble napoleons. Place 1 slice eggplant on plate. Top with a
   cheese slice then a tomato slice. Repeat 2 more times until you have
   3 layers, ending with eggplant.

Tip
●Secure napoleons by sticking fresh rosemary sprigs or wooden skewers
through the top of each stack. Drizzle Italian dressing over eggplant. Serve
immediately.
●You can also top the napoleons with your favorite pasta sauce or combine
some pesto sauce with chicken stock and drizzle over napoleons.

Vegetarian Chili

Makes 4 to 6 servings

Ingredients
1 tablespoon canola oil
1 cup green bell pepper, diced
1 cup red onion, diced
2 tablespoons Spice Delight BBQ Rub
2 cups Morningstar Farms Frozen Soy Crumbs
2 (14.5 oz.) cans diced tomatoes
2 cups vegetable stock
1 (15 oz.) can black beans, rinsed and drained
1 (15 oz.) kidney beans, rinsed and drained

Method
1. Heat oil in a large stockpot over medium heat.
2. Add bell pepper, onion, Spice Delight BBQ Rub, soy crumbs and tomatoes. Cook 5 minutes, stirring often.
3. Stir in vegetable stock and beans. Simmer over low heat 30 minutes, stirring occasionally to prevent sticking.

Tip
To make this meal higher in fiber, serve over brown rice or whole-wheat pasta.

Zucchini Lasagna

This low-carb lasagna is easy to prepare. The use of frozen vegetables makes this an easy and convenient recipe. Normandy style refers to a mix of broccoli and cauliflower florets and cut carrots.

Makes 4 to 6 servings

Ingredients
16 oz. skim or low-fat Ricotta cheese
2 cups frozen Normandy style vegetables, thawed, coarsely chopped
½ lb. button or Portabella mushrooms, sliced thin
¼ cup red onion, diced
½ cup Egg Beaters
1 tablespoon Spice Delight All-Purpose Essence
1 (28 oz.) jar pasta sauce (your favorite)
2 lbs. zucchini squash, cut lengthwise into thin slices
½ cup Parmesan cheese, divided
1 cup part-skim Mozzarella cheese

Method
1. Preheat oven to 350 degrees.
2. Line and 8 x 8-inch baking pan with parchment paper.
3. In a large bowl combine Ricotta, Normandy vegetables, onion, mushrooms, Egg Beaters and Spice Delight All-Purpose Essence. Keep zucchini separate.
4. To assemble the lasagna, first spread ⅓ of the pasta sauce in bottom of pan, next layer ⅓ of the zucchini and ½ of the Ricotta-vegetable mix. Repeat layer. Next layer on remaining zucchini. Top with the remaining ⅓ of sauce.
5. Sprinkle with Parmesan and Mozzarella cheese.
6. Bake 45 to 50 minutes uncovered until cheese is bubbly and edges are slightly brown. Allow lasagna to cool 10 minutes before serving.

Pesto Pizza Bread

This lower fat pizza is delicious as a main entrée with green salad. It is also great as an appetizer when cut into bite-size pieces.

Makes 4 to 6 servings

Ingredients
1 loaf Focaccia bread, cut in half lengthwise
½ cup pesto sauce (your favorite)
1 teaspoon Spice Delight All-Purpose Essence
1 large tomato, sliced thin
½ cup Parmesan cheese

Method
1. Preheat oven to broil.
2. Spread pesto sauce evenly over cut side of bread.
3. Dust Spice Delight All-Purpose Essence evenly over bread.
4. Layer tomatoes over top of bread.
5. Sprinkle Parmesan cheese on top of tomatoes.
6. Place pizza on a cookie sheet. Broil on bottom rack or until cheese has melted and pizza is golden brown, about 3 to 5 minutes.

Tip
To make a Pesto Pizza with Shrimp, slice 6 medium raw shrimp in half, lengthwise, season with Spice Delight All-Purpose Essence and 1 tablespoon olive oil. Sauté shrimp 1 minute per side. Layer shrimp over tomatoes, top with cheese. Continue as directed above.

Veggie Burger Quesadillas

These quesadillas are so good that even a meat-lover will enjoy them.

Makes 2 to 4 servings

Ingredients
2 frozen Morningstar Farms Black Bean Veggie Burgers
2 tablespoons olive oil
¼ cup red onion, diced
2 tablespoons Spice Delight BBQ Rub
1 cup low-fat Mozzarella cheese
1 cup mild salsa
4 corn, wheat or garden vegetable soft tortillas

Method
1. Thaw and dice veggie burgers.
2. In a medium skillet, heat oil over medium heat.
3. Add onion and Spice Delight BBQ Rub. Sauté 3 minutes.
4. Add diced veggie burgers; sauté 3 to 5 minutes until heated through. Remove to a mixing bowl.
5. Place 1 tortilla in pan; spread half of burger mixture, salsa and cheese evenly on top.
6. Top with another tortilla. Cover pan; cook 1 to 2 minutes, then carefully flip. Cook other side 1 to 2 minutes longer.
7. Remove to a serving platter. Let rest for a few minutes before cutting. Cover with foil to keep warm until serving time.
8. Repeat steps 5 to 7 with remaining ingredients.

Tofu Salad

Makes 4 servings

Ingredients

8 oz. extra firm tofu, diced into cubes
½ cup cucumber, thinly sliced
2 teaspoons sweet chili sauce
½ teaspoon fresh grated ginger
2 teaspoons low-sodium teriyaki sauce
2 teaspoons olive oil
½ teaspoon Spice Delight All-Purpose Essence
½ teaspoon prepared mustard
½ teaspoon sesame seeds

Method

1. Place tofu and cucumber in a medium size bowl; set aside.
2. In another bowl, whisk together chili sauce, ginger, teriyaki sauce, olive oil, Spice Delight All-Purpose Essence and mustard.
3. Pour dressing over tofu and cucumbers.
4. Cover and refrigerate for 1 hour.
5. Garnish with sesame seeds at serving time.

Notes:

Chapter 9:
Drinks

This chapter includes an assortment of refreshing drinks. I have included smoothies, teas, flavorful fruity drinks and shakes for your enjoyment.

Chapter 9: Drinks

Citrus Smoothie

Makes 2 servings

Ingredients
1 cup low-fat yogurt
2 cups fresh orange sections, seeds removed
2 tablespoons agave nectar
⅛ teaspoon orange extract
2 sprigs mint leaves to garnish

Method
1. Place yogurt, orange sections, syrup and extract in a blender.
2. Blend until smooth.
3. Pour smoothie in a glass over ice and garnish with mint.

Peanut Butter & Banana Soy Milk Smoothie

Makes 4 to 6 servings

Ingredients
4 very ripe bananas, peeled, cut into ½-inch chunks
12 oz. fat-free vanilla yogurt
½ cup vanilla soy milk
6 ice cubes
¼ cup creamy or crunchy peanut butter

Method
1. Freeze bananas 45 minutes or until firm.
2. After bananas are firm, place them in a blender along with the rest of the ingredients listed above.
3. Blend until mixture is thick and smooth.
4. Serve immediately.

Banana Soy Milk Smoothie

Makes 2 servings

Ingredients
1 large banana, peeled, cut into ½-inch chunks
4 ice cubes
¼ cup vanilla soy milk
⅛ teaspoon ground allspice
2 tablespoons turbinado sugar (sugar in the raw)

Method
1. Freeze banana 45 minutes or until firm.
2. After banana is firm, place them in a blender along with the rest of the ingredients listed above.
3. Blend until mixture is thick and smooth.
4. Serve immediately.

Tip
To get a caramel flavor, do not freeze banana, instead, sauté cut-up banana in 1 teaspoon Smart Balance Butter Substitute over medium heat for 4 minutes per side or until the natural sugars start to brown and become caramelized.

Lemon Mint Tea

This cooling and refreshing tea tastes great on a hot summer day or after a good workout at the gym.

Makes 8 servings

Ingredients
8 cups spring or filtered water
6 peppermint tea bags
1 cup turbinado sugar (sugar in the raw)
¼ cup fresh lemon juice

Method
1. In a large pot, bring water to a boil and turn off heat.
2. Add tea bags and steep for 10 minutes.
3. Remove tea bags; stir in sugar.
4. Pour tea into pitcher; stir in lemon juice.
5. Let cool and serve over ice.

Alfalfa Mint Tea

The mint in this tea is soothing to the soul and the digestive system. The health benefits of the alfalfa, including vitamins and minerals, make it refreshingly good for you.

Makes 4 to 6 servings

Ingredients
32 oz. spring or filtered water
4 oz. alfalfa tea leaves
4 oz. peppermint tea leaves
Honey to taste

Method
1. Bring water to a boil and turn off heat. Add the tea leaves.
2. Steep alfalfa and peppermint tea leaves for 10 minutes.
3. Strain into a pitcher to remove tea leaves.
4. Stir in honey to desired sweetness. Let cool and serve over ice.

Tip
You can add a splash of fresh lemon or lime juice to brighten up the flavors of this summertime treat.

Ginger Mint Tea

Ginger and mint are great teas for stomach upset, but this tea also makes a nice refreshing drink, served hot or cold.

Makes 2 quarts

Ingredients
2 quarts spring water
1-inch ginger root, thinly sliced
4 bags peppermint tea
¼ cup raw brown turbinado sugar (sugar in the raw)
¼ cup agave syrup (natural sweetener)
2 mint leaves to garnish

Method
1. In a large stockpot; bring spring water to a boil.
2. Add ginger; boil for 3 minutes.
3. Turn heat off, add tea bags and steep for 5 minutes.
4. Strain into pitcher to remove ginger solids.
5. Sweeten with sugar and syrup to taste.
6. To serve chilled; refrigerate, then pour into tea glasses filled with ice and garnish with mint leaves.
7. To serve hot; do not chill after straining. Pour into a mug and garnish with mint leaves.

Sweet Orange Tea

This tea was first introduced to me by Keith Gaither, a fellow chef, when we worked together at the famous Village Tavern in Winston-Salem, North Carolina.

Makes 4 to 6 servings

Ingredients
32 oz. spring water
4 tea bags (black or orange pekoe)
Dark brown sugar to taste
Juice of 6 sweet oranges

Method
1. Bring water to a boil and turn off heat.
2. Let tea bags steep for 5 minutes.
3. Remove tea bags and sweeten to taste with brown sugar.
4. Add orange juice; stir.
5. Chill and enjoy.

Tip
If tea is not sweet enough it will not bring out that great orange flavor. Try using orange extract to give you a deeper orange flavor.

Orange-Grape Drink

This strange combination is a childhood favorite that I still love to drink.

Makes 2 to 4 servings

Ingredients
16 oz. Welch's purple grape juice
8 oz. Tropicana orange juice
2 tablespoons dark brown sugar

Method
1. Place all of the listed ingredients in a pitcher.
2. Mix well until sugar has dissolved.
3. Chill and serve over ice.

Sorrell Ginger Drink

The West Indies is known for this great drink. Sorrell can be purchased in Mexican supermarkets. It is sometimes called "Jamaican flower" and has a pretty burgundy color. It comes dried and its flavor is a combination of raspberry and strawberry.

Makes 4 to 6 servings

Ingredients
32 oz. spring or filtered water
2 cups dried Sorrell flowers
1 teaspoon fresh ginger, peeled and chopped
Turbinado sugar to taste (sugar in the raw)

Method
1. In a large stockpot, combine water, Sorrell and ginger; bring to a boil for 10 minutes.
2. Turn off heat and let stand for 10 minutes longer.
3. Strain drink; discard Sorrell and ginger.
4. Sweeten to taste with turbinado sugar.

Tip
You can add some sparkling water to give this drink some fizz. You can also add a splash of orange juice to give this drink a little citrus flavor.

Apple-Lime Splash

Limes and brown sugar give this apple drink a tropical splash.

Makes 2 servings

Ingredients
2 limes
16 oz. unsweetened apple juice or apple cider
Dark brown sugar to taste

Method
1. Roll limes on hard surface to help release the juice.
2. Cut limes in half; juice in citrus juicer.
3. Pour apple juice into a pitcher. Stir in lime juice.
4. Sweeten Apple-Lime Splash to taste with brown sugar.

Fruit Punch

This all-natural punch will become a hit with the entire family! Unlike store-bought fruit punch you control the sugar content and sweetness of this punch.

Makes 8 to 10 servings

Ingredients
24 oz. no-sugar added apple juice or cider, chilled
12 oz. no-sugar added cranberry juice, chilled
12 oz. orange juice, chilled
Dark brown sugar to taste
1 orange, sliced thin to garnish

Method
1. Mix the apple, cranberry and orange juices in a large punch bowl.
2. Sweeten punch to taste with brown sugar.
3. Garnish punch with sliced orange.

Tip
Add some sparkling water for fizz.

Orange Bellini

This fruity, fizzy drink can be enjoyed by the entire family. To create a version of the Italian adult cocktail that inspired this wonderful drink, use champagne instead of sparkling water.

Makes 4 to 6 servings

Ingredients
¾ cup orange or tangerine juice
½ cup frozen peaches, thawed
2 tablespoons agave nectar or pure maple syrup
⅛ teaspoon ground cinnamon
3 drops orange extract
4 oz. sparkling water
Several orange or tangerine segments to garnish

Method
1. Place fruit juice, peaches, syrup, cinnamon and extract in a blender or food processor and blend until smooth.
2. Add 2 ounces sparkling water or champagne to each glass.
3. Evenly divide the fruit juice mixture into each glass and garnish with orange segments.

Cranberry-Lime Mocktail

This drink makes a wonderfully refreshing non-alcoholic cocktail!

Makes 2 servings

Ingredients
Juice of 2 limes
2 tablespoons turbinado sugar (sugar in the raw)
16 oz. cranberry juice

Method
1. Place the lime juice, sugar and cranberry juice in a pitcher; mix until sugar has dissolved.
2. Serve chilled over ice.

Tip
You can add a little ginger ale soda and make this a fizzy party drink.

Limeade

Limes are used a lot for tropical drinks. This drink will make you feel transported to your own little oasis.

Makes 2 servings

Ingredients
Juice of 3 limes
⅓ cup turbinado sugar (sugar in the raw)
3 drops Angostura Aromatic Bitters
16 oz. spring or filtered water

Method
1. Place lime juice in pitcher.
2. Add sugar and bitters.
3. Stir in water until sugar dissolves.

Ginger Limeade

Makes 8 to 12 servings

Ingredients

6 cups spring or filtered water
½ cup turbinado sugar (sugar in the raw)
3 tablespoons fresh ginger, peeled and chopped
¼ cup fresh lime juice

Method

1. Place the first 3 ingredients in a large pot and bring to a boil. Boil for 5 minutes.
2. Strain into a pitcher to remove ginger solids; stir in lime juice. Let cool and serve over ice.

Banana Chocolate Shake

This is my favorite shake. I love chocolate and banana together in any form.

Makes 2 servings

Ingredients
½ cup whole milk
1 large ripe banana, quartered
1 oz. Hershey's milk chocolate bar
1 ¾ cup premium chocolate ice cream

Method
1. Place all of the ingredients in a blender.
2. Pulse a few times, then blend on high speed until shake is smooth and creamy.
3. Serve immediately.

Strawberry Shake

The fresh fruit base in this recipe is not only nutritious but also delicious!

Makes 2 servings

Ingredients
Fruit Base
1 lb. fresh strawberries, hulls removed, quartered
6 tablespoons turbinado sugar (sugar in the raw)
3 tablespoons strawberry jam
2 teaspoons fresh lemon juice
Shake
¼ to ½ cup whole milk
1 ¾ cups premium strawberry ice cream

Method
1. In a large skillet over medium heat, add the strawberries, sugar, jam and lemon juice to make fruit base.
2. Bring to a boil and then reduce to a simmer and cook base for 20 minutes.
3. Let fruit base cool.
4. Place ¼ cup of the fruit base along with the milk and strawberry ice cream in a blender. Reserve remaining fruit base for later use.
5. Pulse a few times, then blend on high speed until shake is smooth and creamy.
6. Serve immediately.

Peach-Cinnnamon Shake

When fresh peaches are out of season, you can use frozen peaches.

Makes 2 servings

Ingredients
Fruit Base
1 lb. fresh or frozen peaches, quartered
6 tablespoons turbinado sugar (sugar in the raw)
3 tablespoons peach jam
2 teaspoons fresh lemon juice
1 teaspoon ground cinnamon
Shake
¼ to ½ cup whole milk
1 ¾ cups premium peach or vanilla ice cream

Method
1. In a large skillet over medium heat, add peaches, sugar, jam, lemon juice and cinnamon to make fruit base.
2. Bring to a boil and then reduce to a simmer and cook base for 20 minutes.
3. Let fruit base cool.
4. Place ¼ cup of the fruit base along with the milk and ice cream in a blender. Reserve remaining fruit base for later use.
5. Pulse a few times, then blend on high speed until shake is smooth and creamy.
6. Serve immediately.

Peanut Butter Banana and Chocolate Shake

Makes 2 servings

Ingredients
½ cup whole milk
1 large ripe banana, quartered
3 heaping tablespoons creamy peanut butter
2 oz. Hershey's milk chocolate bar
1 ¾ cup premium vanilla ice cream

Method
1. Place all of the ingredients in a blender.
2. Pulse a few times, then blend on high speed until shake is smooth and creamy.
3. Serve immediately.

Notes:

Chapter 10:
Sweets

This chapter is dedicated to all of the wonderful, sweet, sticky, delicious treats that comfort us, help us celebrate and refresh us. Many of my own childhood memories played a part in helping me to develop some of these recipes. The use of fresh, healthy ingredients transforms some of the recipes from just good to good for you. So indulge and enjoy, but remember the key to a well-balanced life is all things in moderation.

Chapter 10: Sweets

Pan-Fried Plantains

This banana-like fruit needs to be cooked to bring out the flavor. Plantains are a staple in Hispanic and West Indies households.

Makes 2 to 4 servings

Ingredients
¼ cup turbinado sugar (sugar in the raw)
1 teaspoon ground cinnamon
1 tablespoon Smart Balance Butter Substitute
2 ripe plantains, peeled and sliced ½-inch thick

Method
1. Mix sugar and cinnamon in a small bowl; set aside.
2. Melt butter substitute over medium heat in a medium sauté pan.
3. Dip both sides of cut plantains in sugar mixture.
4. Sauté plantains for 3 minutes per side or until golden brown.

Tip
Serve with ice cream or dust with powdered sugar and eat as a snack.

Apple Tart

Makes 4 to 6 servings

Ingredients

2 tablespoons unsalted butter
3 Granny Smith apples, peeled, cored, thinly sliced
¼ cup packed brown sugar
1 teaspoon ground cinnamon
Juice of a fresh lemon half
¼ cup dark raisins
Pinch of sea salt
1 refrigerated Pillsbury rolled pie crust
1 sheet parchment paper
¼ cup chopped pecans

Method

1. Preheat oven to 350 degrees.
2. In a large skillet over medium heat, melt butter and add the next 6 ingredients.
3. Cook 10 minutes or until apples are soft, stirring occasionally.
4. Place pie crust on parchment paper lined rimmed cookie sheet.
5. Pinch and turn up edge of pie crust to form a rim to hold filling.
6. Use a slotted spoon to add apple filling to pie crust. Sprinkle with chopped pecans.
7. Bake 15 to 20 minutes or until crust is golden brown.

Sweet Potato Pancakes with Maple Syrup

These pancakes taste great with the turbinado sugar and pure vanilla extract.

Makes 2 to 4 servings

Ingredients
½ cup Bruce's Sweet Potato Pancake Mix
⅓ cup spring water
1 tablespoon turbinado sugar (sugar in the raw)
¼ teaspoon pure vanilla extract
¼ cup pure maple syrup
2 tablespoons Smart Balance Butter Substitute

Method
1. In a medium size bowl, add first 4 ingredients listed above; mix well.
2. Cook pancakes about 3 minutes per side over medium heat.
3. When done, add syrup and butter substitute.

Tip
Bruce's Sweet Potato Pancake Mix can be found at The Fresh Market.

Maple Almond Butter Bites

Makes 2 to 4 servings

Ingredients
4 slices multi-grain bread
2 tablespoons almond butter
2 tablespoons pure maple syrup
2 teaspoons dark raisins

Method
1. Spread almond butter and maple syrup on 1 side of 2 slices of bread.
2. Sprinkle 1 teaspoon raisins on top of almond butter.
3. Top with remaining slices of bread.
4. Cut into squares and serve.

Tip
Before you cut sandwiches into squares, you can toast sandwiches in toaster oven.

Pan-Fried Plums with Port Wine

Makes 2 to 4 servings

Ingredients

2 tablespoons turbinado sugar (sugar in the raw)
1 teaspoon ground cinnamon
4 large plums, pitted and quartered
1 tablespoon Smart Balance Butter Substitute
¼ cup port wine

Method

1. Mix sugar and cinnamon in a small bowl; set aside.
2. Place plums in medium size bowl; sprinkle enough sugar mix to lightly coat them. Reserve leftover mix for later use.
3. Melt butter substitute over medium heat in a medium sauté pan.
4. Sauté plums for 3 minutes, stirring occasionally.
5. Add port wine; cook 2 minutes longer.

Tip

Serve plums over pound cake.

Pan-Fried Peaches with Bourbon

Makes 2 to 4 servings

Ingredients

1 tablespoon Smart Balance Butter Substitute
2 large ripe peaches, pitted and diced medium (about 2 cups)
3 tablespoons turbinado sugar (sugar in the raw)
⅛ teaspoon ground cinnamon
¼ cup bourbon
2 scoops French vanilla ice cream

Method

1. Heat large pan with butter substitute over medium high heat.
2. Add peaches, sugar and cinnamon.
3. Sauté for 3 to 5 minutes, until peaches are caramel in color.
4. Add bourbon; cook 1 minute.
5. Pour mixture over ice cream.

Tip

You can also add chopped pecans, walnuts or almonds on top of this dessert.

Pan-Fried Peaches with Pound Cake & Ice Cream

Makes 2 servings

Ingredients

2 cups peaches, pitted and cut into 8 chunks
2 tablespoons turbinado sugar (sugar in the raw)
1 teaspoon ground cinnamon
1 tablespoon unsalted butter
2 slices vanilla pound cake
2 scoops vanilla ice cream
Whipped cream for garnish
1 tablespoon chopped pecans for garnish
2 whole fresh strawberries for garnish

Method

1. Place peaches in a medium size bowl.
2. Mix sugar and cinnamon together.
3. Sprinkle sugar mix over peaches; mix well so that sugar mix coats peaches evenly.
4. Heat skillet over medium heat.
5. Add butter; cook peaches for about 10 minutes until peaches are caramel in color, stirring occasionally.
6. To assemble dessert, place pound cake on bottom of bowl. Top pound cake with ice cream. Top ice cream with peaches and desired amount of whipped cream.
7. Garnish with pecans and strawberries.

Pan-Fried Bananas with Ice Cream

After the first bite of this dessert, your words will be "It's delicious!"

Makes 2 servings

Ingredients
2 tablespoons turbinado sugar (sugar in the raw)
1 teaspoon ground cinnamon
1 tablespoon Smart Balance Butter Substitute
2 large bananas, sliced ½-inch thick
2 scoops vanilla ice cream
1 tablespoon chopped pecans to garnish

Method
1. Mix sugar and cinnamon in a small bowl; set aside.
2. Melt butter substitute over medium heat in a medium sauté pan.
3. Dip both sides of cut bananas in sugar mixture.
4. Sauté bananas for 3 minutes per side or until golden brown.
5. Place scoops of ice cream in a dessert bowl, top with bananas. Sprinkle on pecans to garnish.

Tip
Try pouring this over banana nut bread or pound cake.

Grits Pudding

Cooking grits in milk or cream makes them thick and creamy. This is the ultimate comfort food.

Makes 6 to 8 servings

Ingredients

4 ½ cups whole milk
¾ cup turbinado sugar (sugar in the raw)
1 teaspoon sea salt
1 teaspoon ground cinnamon
½ teaspoon vanilla extract
1 cup quick grits

Method

In a large stockpot over medium heat, add the first 5 ingredients. Bring to a boil. Stir in grits. Cover and reduce heat to simmer. Cook grits 30 minutes or until done, stirring often to prevent sticking.

Rice Pudding

I have great memories of my mother making this pudding with leftover rice. It's creamy and delicious.

Makes 4 servings

Ingredients
2 cups water
2 teaspoons unsalted butter
2 cups whole milk
2 cups low-fat half & half
1 cup turbinado sugar (sugar in the raw)
½ cup dark raisins
½ vanilla bean, cut in half or ½ teaspoon vanilla extract
1 cup Arborio or short grain rice
Ground cinnamon to garnish
Mint leaves to garnish

Method
1. Combine all ingredients listed above in a medium size saucepan, except rice, cinnamon and mint.
2. Bring mixture to a boil; stir in rice.
3. Turn heat to a simmer. Cook 35 minutes uncovered, until rice is tender, stirring often to prevent sticking.
4. Remove from heat; let rice cool. It will thicken as it cools. Serve warm or chilled.
5. Divide among dessert dishes. Dust with cinnamon and garnish with a mint leaf.

Nutella & Banana Sandwich

This unique sandwich will become a hit with children as well as adults. Nutella is a European hazelnut chocolate spread you can find in the grocery store with peanut butter and jelly.

Makes 2 to 4 servings

Ingredients
4 slices fresh raisin bread
2 tablespoons Nutella Hazelnut Spread
2 bananas, sliced thin

Method
1. Spread 1 tablespoon Nutella on 1 side of 2 slices of raisin bread.
2. Layer sliced banana on top of Nutella.
3. Top sandwiches with remaining raisin bread.

Almond Butter & Maple Syrup Sandwich

This is like a peanut butter and jelly sandwich, but it tastes much better and it is better for you because this sandwich is all natural.

Makes 2 to 4 servings

Ingredients
4 slices whole-grain bread
2 tablespoons almond butter
2 tablespoons pure maple syrup

Method
1. Spread 1 tablespoon almond butter on 1 side of bread.
2. Spread 1 tablespoon maple syrup on top of almond butter.
3. Top sandwich with remaining bread slices.

Orange Flavored Whipped Cream

Adding Grand Marnier, the orange flavored liqueur, can further enhance this whipped cream.

Makes 4 servings

Ingredients
1 cup cold heavy cream
2 tablespoons confectioners' sugar (powdered sugar)
⅛ teaspoon pure orange extract
1 tablespoon Grand Marnier orange flavored liqueur (optional)

Method
1. Place cream, sugar and extract (and liqueur, if desired) in a cold glass or stainless steel bowl.
2. Using a hand mixer or stand mixer, whip all of the ingredients on high speed until soft and creamy. Don't overbeat.

Tip
If you want to make orange butter, keep whipping until cream starts to become solid. It may appear to be curdled. Drain liquid that separates out and discard. Butter is ready to use.

Vanilla Flavored Whipped Cream

This simple whipped cream can be used to top ice cream sundaes, milk shakes or pound cakes.

Makes 4 servings

Ingredients
1 cup cold heavy cream
2 tablespoons confectioners' sugar (powdered sugar)
½ teaspoon pure vanilla extract

Method
1. Place cream, sugar and extract in a cold glass or stainless steel bowl.
2. Using a hand mixer or stand mixer, whip all of the ingredients on high speed until soft and creamy. Don't overbeat.

Tip
Add ground cinnamon, nutmeg or a little ground ginger to some whipped cream to compliment the dessert you are topping.

Orange Sherbet Ice Pops

This sherbet takes me back to my childhood. The Good Humor ice cream truck would come by our house with that great vanilla ice cream and orange flavored ice pops.

Makes 4 servings

Ingredients
2 cups non-fat skim milk
2 cups low-fat plain or vanilla yogurt
1 cup frozen orange juice concentrate
⅔ cup turbinado sugar (sugar in the raw)
⅛ teaspoon orange extract

Method
1. Place milk, yogurt, juice concentrate, sugar and extract in a blender.
2. Blend until smooth.
3. To make ice pops: pour mixture in Popsicle molds per manufacturer's instructions and freeze.
4. To make sherbet: pour mixture into any type of airtight container and freeze for 3 to 4 hours or until firm.

Bread Pudding

Bread pudding is one of my favorite comfort food desserts. It's easy to make and great with a little whipped cream and strawberries on top.

Makes 4 to 6 servings

Ingredients
4 cups stale bread or pastry, cubed
2 cups dark raisins
2 cups whole milk
1 cup low-fat half & half
3 large eggs, beaten
1 ½ cups packed brown sugar
1 tablespoon ground cinnamon
1 teaspoon vanilla extract
1 teaspoon rum extract
½ cup chopped nuts (optional)
Garnish: whipped cream and fresh sliced strawberries

Method
1. Preheat oven to 350 degrees 15 minutes prior to baking.
2. In an 8 x 8-inch square baking pan, combine cubed bread and raisins; set aside.
3. In a separate bowl, add the remaining ingredients,; mix well.
4. Pour mixture over bread and raisins. Spread in an even layer.
5. Cover and refrigerate 30 minutes.
6. Bake uncovered 40 to 45 minutes or until golden brown and custard is set. Do not overbake.
7. Garnish with whipped cream and strawberries.

Notes: